Greenest good wishes

Patricia   2011.

DOWN TO EARTH

A beginner's guide to the
healthiest food you will ever produce

Patricia C Parr

DOWN TO EARTH

All Rights Reserved

© MMXI by Patricia C Parr

This book may not be reproduced in whole or in part, by any means, without written consent of the publisher.

Published by Down To Earth Books

Email: pcparr@btinternet.com

ISBN: 978-0-9568812-0-5
Cover : Lloyd Arbour
Layout: Lloyd Arbour
Edit: AllIvy Editing Services

COMPANIES, ORGANIZATIONS, INSTITUTIONS, AND INDUSTRY PUBLICATIONS:
Quantity discounts are available on bulk purchases of this book for reselling, educational purposes, subscription incentives, gifts, sponsorship, or fundraising. For more information, please contact our Special Sales Department at Down To Earth Books.

Contents

Foreword		7
Introduction		11
Chapter 1	*The Scary Bit: Just What Are We Eating?*	15
Chapter 2	*Organics to the Rescue*	23
Chapter 3	*Beat the Jargon*	35
Chapter 4	*But I Don't Have a Garden: How to Use the Space You Do Have*	47
Chapter 5	*Getting Started*	67
Chapter 6	*A Child Could Do It: Herbs and Salad*	95
Chapter 7	*Social Climbers: Peas and Beans*	121
Chapter 8	*Back to Your Roots*	141
Chapter 9	*Being Greens*	157
Chapter 10	*Away You Go: The Gardening Year*	173
Appendix 1	*Beneficial Additions to Help Growth*	189
Appendix 2	*Coping Organically with Pests and Diseases*	195

DOWN TO EARTH

Foreword

Daily we are cajoled, urged and warned to save ourselves from ourselves. All branches of the media describe our certain doom by global warming, climate change, carbon emissions, rising sea levels, and air and water pollution, while various governments make noble-sounding promises either to avert or stem these man-made phenomena. Genetically modified foods are simultaneously promoted as the way ahead as well as presenting risks to consumers and the environment with too many unknowns. Al Gore's *An Inconvenient Truth* has an inescapable, apocalyptic message.

It is easy to feel too small to make any kind of effective difference until we realise that it is only on an individual basis that something big will be accomplished, because all the fine political statements and agreements have achieved nothing.

Organic produce, however, is slowly gaining popularity and availability. Farmers' markets and food fairs are increasingly in demand and well attended. The green scene is strengthening. Organic products are now an option in supermarkets. There are waiting lists for allotments. The media has raised our collective awareness about additives.

It appears that we are trying to tackle these issues individually. Many of us think we ought to grow our own food but fear we haven't either the knowledge or space to do so.

Patricia Parr's *Down to Earth* is exactly the handbook every gardener, from seasoned propagator to idealistic novice, needs. In clear language the reader is given an enlightened, straight-forward guide to growing safe food for healthy eating. It demystifies all aspects of vegetable growing, and removes the difficult science and Frankenstein food elements, putting the reader in charge, thus inspiring the gardener.

Her book will give you sensible strategies for producing what you want to eat, when you want it, and, crucially, open your eyes to the potential space and light for growing, no matter how limited both seem. A by-product of all these positive points is that your individual garden will save you from expensive gym memberships, over-flowing wheelie bins and horticultural myths and will also benefit the planet.

Do we need another book about growing our own vegetables? Haven't we already had a surplus of television programmes with accompanying texts on the subject? Clearly the answer to these questions is first an emphatic "Yes!" and then "No!". This book is realistic and practical for the first-time gardener of any age. Most importantly for the twenty-first century gardener, it does so in an entirely eco-friendly way.

With humour, enthusiasm and common sense in a refreshingly welcome style, we learn that beans are beautiful and that the bean trench need not be a mystery, that many vegetables can be grown in pots, that you don't need an orchard, merely a suitable container for fruit trees and only a hanging basket for strawberries. A bonus of these methods is that you will save your knees and back by gardening this way while creating and managing your green spaces.

Finally, in using Patricia's easy-to-follow plans, you will provide yourself with vegetables and fruit that are safe for you and safe for the environment. Your health and that of the earth will benefit. What's not to be gained? "Down to Earth" indeed.

- Joy Howard

Independent Tree Warden,
working with Plymouth City Council.

May 2009

DOWN TO EARTH

Introduction

I was very fortunate to be introduced to organic gardening at a very early age (eight or so). At the time, I didn't know it was organic – it was just the way things were done then.

Growing up in a working-class area, where there was little spare money, meant that everyone used what they had, what they could make or what they could scrounge for free. We all saved things and reused them rather than buying new or throwing away; we didn't know it was recycling – we called it "thrifty" and "common-sense".

So, as a child, I considered it quite normal that our neighbours would be out on the road with a shovel and bucket after the rag and bone man's horse had left a nice pile of manure behind. After having the chimney swept, the sweep always asked, "Do you want the soot?" It was dumped in a special corner, underneath the mock orange bush and spread around the garden later, after it had got nice and wet. I knew it did the plants good and kept pests away, but didn't learn why till very much later.

When I had my own gardens, I automatically grew things the way I had been taught as a child. I knew no other way. So all my gardening life I have been "green" without knowing it!

Now, organic gardening—protecting the environment, being green—is becoming fashionable. This is no bad thing if it makes more people aware of good growing practices and having a sustainable planet. The downside is that it has become technical, full of jargon and something of a crusade, which can put people off.

Quite a lot of people are becoming concerned about how our food is produced and are looking for a safe and sure source. For me, because I have always done it, the logical solution is to produce your food yourself. That way, you know exactly what you are eating.

> **Sermon No. 1:**
> Home-grown food is fresher, better tasting and healthier than anything you will buy, anywhere. So there!

So how do I start?

Even with the desire to eat healthier, it may not come naturally to you. So, first, some general tips.

1. **Start small.**

   Taking on an allotment or large garden from scratch can be really daunting if you have little or no experience. You might work up to that eventually, but start off with just a few items, in whatever space you have now, to get a feel, and more importantly, a taste, of your own produce.

2. **Use what space you have**.

   Even if you don't have a garden, you can grow something. Grow fresh herbs from seed on a window ledge. A balcony or small paved/concrete patch can hold a few pots. Containers can be hung from railings, and plant pots can march up a flight of steps. See what you can find.

3. **Think organic right from the start**.

   Adopt the principles (see chapter 2), and adapt them to your space and needs.

4. **Recycle.**

   Much of the equipment you will use can have been something else previously. We will go into more detail later (chapter 6), but, for now, consider yoghurt pots, egg boxes or trays, toilet roll middles, even old CDs. Keep reading; all will be revealed.

5. **Apply common sense at all times**.

   Most growing is a matter of following simple instructions and applying them to your particular needs and lifestyle. If it feels right for you and works for the plants (and you will see when they are unhappy), it's OK. I shall not be giving you instructions which are readily available on seed packets (e.g. type of plant, when to sow); you can read those for yourself.

So do join me in this gentle adventure. You will probably have some fun, and you will certainly benefit from what you produce. In fact, there is a risk that you will end up quite pleased with yourself.

Warning!

Growing your own crops can become addictive! You may intend to keep to just a few lettuce in a pot, but you could end up with an allotment (or small field, in my case). YOU HAVE BEEN WARNED!

DOWN TO EARTH

CHAPTER ONE

The Scary Bit:
Just What Are We Eating?

CHAPTER
 ONE

Most people, most of the time, don't really think about what they are eating. By that, I mean that whilst they will choose peas or carrots with a meal or decide on chops or mince today, they do not ask where the items came from or how they were grown.

In recent years, there has been a growing awareness of the science of food, and more and more groups are proclaiming the value or organic growing. But why should this be any healthier than other methods of growing? To give you a real view of how most food is grown in western "civilisation", we need to go back to the early 1900s.

Fasten your seat belts, readers; it's going to be a bumpy ride!

How most food is grown

In the twentieth century, populations grew quickly, largely thanks to improved medical and health facilities. There was a need for farmers to produce more food, preferably quickly and cheaply.

Crops will only produce in relation to the amount of food they absorb; poor soil produces poor yields. The secret of heavy production is fertiliser – lots of it. Good, old-fashioned manure is an excellent additive. It is slow to work, stays in the soil, and is available on most farms in some quantity or other.

But if you want more and you want it quickly, you need something which will get into the soil in a fraction of the time and is much lighter to handle than the cartloads of farm manure.

Fortunately, clever scientists had just the thing: artificial fertilisers based on nitrates and phosphates. These could be produced quickly and cheaply, were easy to apply being in powder form and worked a treat, increasing yields and profits.

Governments liked the new fertilisers, too, and encouraged farmers to use them. They could see a future of cheap, plentiful food. So, most farmers adopted the new fertilisers. It was an easy system with visible results.

The rise of the worriers

In the 1930s, some far-sighted horticulturalists began to feel concern about the use of chemical fertilisers. They were uneasy about the chances of the chemicals accumulating in the soil, whether this would do any harm to the soil in the long term, whether it would affect the environment generally.

Some growers banded together to monitor the long-term effects of artificial fertilisers and to compare them to their own growing methods, based on the older and more basic practices. They called themselves the Soil Association (www.soilassociation.org.uk) and they checked soil, content of crops, watercourses and aquatic life, bird numbers—in fact, anything which might be affected by what goes into soil.

Just after World War II, a practical offshoot of the Soil Association was set up, the Henry Doubleday Organic Association (www.gardenorganic.org.uk), to begin actively testing and recording methods of growing which are now known everywhere as "organic". Both groups are in the forefront of the move towards healthier food growing. Their years of work have produced some disturbing statistics.

It says a lot for these pioneers that they were prepared to stand up to the huge corporations who produced quick, cheap chemicals for farmers. Their message that the quick fix of increased cropping and fewer pests was a potentially dangerous situation was not very welcome to most farmers. The even longer term message that prolonged usage would cause heavy, possibly terminal damage to the soil and the food chain was considered cranky and alarmist.

Now, seventy years on, we are beginning to see the results. *And the cranks were right!*

What are they worrying about?

1. Our health

The first and most obvious criticism of using artificial chemicals on fruit and vegetables is that the chemicals go into the plants and the plants go into us. There is little evidence that cooking reduces the chemical content, so we eat however much chemical is in the plant. Each time we eat a sprayed fruit or vegetable, we are taking in a little bit of chemical. Every day, every meal.

A really scary fact is that food producers do not only use fertilisers to encourage their crops. Fruit and vegetables are regularly sprayed with chemical pesticides, herbicides and fungicides to control any pests, weeds or diseases which may attack the crop. No one really knows how all these chemicals react with each other or what they are adding to the plant. And then we eat it!

Recent research is showing that the accumulation of chemicals in our bodies may well be the cause of a number of serious health problems. There may be a direct link with the increase in cancers, heart problems and allergies, and possibly more.

> If you really want to scare yourself with horrid statistics about the chemicals in fresh produce, check out the DEFRA website: www.defra.gov.uk/farm/acu/research/reports/nf0422.pdf.

Secondly, it has been shown by a number of researchers that all fruit and vegetables begin to lose their vitamin content from the moment they are harvested. This process is natural and inevitable. The rate of loss is steady, so the longer the produce is stored, the more content will be lost.

As vitamins are one of the major benefits we get from fresh produce, it is sensible to eat the food as soon as possible after harvest. Straight from the garden is about as fresh as it gets.

The same research has shown the presence of "trace elements" in fruit and vegetables, such as zinc, iron and potassium. Although only needed in small quantities, these trace elements are very important to human health. They encourage the natural immune system to work and keep the blood flow healthy, amongst other benefits. Trace elements are markedly less in commercially grown food, where chemical growth stimulants have been used.

Everybody needs a set quantity of vitamins, minerals and trace elements every day. We get them from our food. Obviously, if the produce we eat has a reduced beneficial content due to the conditions by which it was grown, and it has been harvested and stored for some time, that content will be less than adequate. In order to ensure we get sufficient benefit, the simple solution would be to eat much more produce.

Parents of young children will know how difficult it is to persuade them to eat fruit and (particularly) vegetables. Can you imagine the fun you would have getting them to eat twice or three times the quantity? Organically grown really fresh fruit and vegetables can reduce the hassle.

2. Our world

The publicity about global warming started the trend, and now most people are becoming aware of the potential damage man is doing to the environment and the planet. We are constantly reminded of our "carbon footprint", the ozone layer, fish stocks and any number of potential threats to the planet.

A number of established movements are supporting a new environmental approach. These include my own, the Women's Institute. The W.I. has always supported the more organic and natural approach, in essence, but are now actively promoting to, and through, the membership. They are not alone. What few realise is that the damage to the planet starts at a much smaller but more immediate level – the soil itself. The very structure of the soil is contributing to global warming, thanks to the usage of nitrogen fertilisers.

Nitrogen fertiliser makes soil more acidic. To offset this, farmers add lime. Together, the two produce carbon dioxide, which is released into the air. Also, the fertilisers reduce the natural micro-organisms in the soil which break down methane. This allows more methane into the atmosphere than would happen if the organisms could do their work.

All by itself, nitrogen fertiliser adds the two main greenhouse gases into the air, helping the increase in global warming.

At a local level, many areas have seen their streams and rivers polluted by the leaching of chemicals from farmland. In some cases (e.g. the Thames, in the south, and the Rother, in Yorkshire), the rivers have been completely killed. Pesticides have reduced insects and with them birds, hedgehogs, frogs, and other natural predators.

Recent history has shown us the results of short-term growing solutions, carried out without thought to long-term effects. The American Midwest's Dust Bowl and the widening of the Ethiopian deserts are both direct results of short-term farming practices which fed the people for a while but did not feed the land for future growing.

Increasingly, sustainability is becoming a significant factor. It is sensible to grow crops today in a way which will enable the soil to produce more crops tomorrow.

DOWN TO EARTH

CHAPTER TWO

Organics to the Rescue

CHAPTER TWO

What is organic?

Strictly speaking, organic growing started in medieval times, when the average peasant ploughed, sowed and harvested his small patch, fed it with dung from the family cow or pig and prayed for a good harvest.

The organic movement, as we know it, is much more recent. In the last ten years, it has become positively fashionable, in the spirit at least, if not in the practice. In some quarters, organic growing has almost become a new age religion. The rules are strict – what you can and cannot use, for example – and hell awaits the miscreant who does not grow correctly!

This, of course, is a lot of nonsense. Organic growing represents a different attitude and approach rather than a set of rules. It assumes that common sense will apply and that everyone is free to choose how they apply the principles to their own projects.

There are guidelines available through organisations in many countries. These are geared to the climate and conditions of that country. It may be called biodynamics or permaculture, but all work to the same principles.

> **Sermon No. 2:**
> Organic does not mean no work, either. Planting seeds then ignoring them and hoping to get a crop is neglect, not growing organically. Yes, some work is involved, but no more than growing any other way. If you start off and stay growing organically, the work will actually lessen with time.
> Organic does mean growing in sympathy and with the co-operation of nature. Growers are gradually realising that it is possible to produce adequate crops without dependence on chemicals; and these crops are healthier to the people who eat them and fairer to the environment.

Organic principles

The basis of all organic thought and practice is the soil. All living plants need the soil to provide an anchor, food and water. The organic gardener tries to produce soil which is as healthy and robust as it can be and to do so using organic matter and time rather than chemicals.

Soil is a living medium and naturally contains a good collection of creatures and organisms which produce usable, valuable content to help crops grow. Organic methods help these creatures keep the soil healthy. It is like people – if you are healthy and vibrant, you do not get so many illnesses or diseases and can cope better with any nasties which come your way.

Organic growing also takes a wider view of protection for the general environment. This is not just from some do-gooding, protectionist reason, but because wildlife – birds, insects, small mammals – can actually help us as much as we help them.

In order to help and protect the soil and, therefore, the environment, organic gardeners try not to use poisonous substances. If, as a last resort, some form of pest or disease control is needed, natural substances are used, which are generally more specific to the problem and so less wide-ranging in their effects.

One must a bit careful of the word "natural" – it can cover some fairly powerful chemicals which can be harmful (like a shark; just because it's natural, it doesn't mean it's safe!) One obvious example is nicotine. This is a plant product and very effective in killing aphids (blackfly). Unfortunately it also kills many other flying insects, including the good ones. AND, it is absorbed by the plant it is sprayed on and so gets into the consumer. It is no longer encouraged!

Some natural chemicals, such as Bordeaux mixture (see appendix 1), are permitted because they are relatively safe to the soil. But the rule of thumb is always – ONLY WHEN ABSOLUTELY NECESSARY!

Usually we try to find another way round major problems. Let me tell you the story of the slugs:

My previous garden was made from scratch (uncultivated, rough ground), and was organic from the beginning. Having cleared the growing area, the first crop planted was potatoes. They grew very well until they were about half-size, but then they began dying very quickly. There were some signs of slug damage, so the plants were checked in the evening with the help of a torch – the plot was alive! I have never seen so many slugs in one place; it was a slug convention!

It would have been very simple to scatter quantities of slug pellets everywhere and this would have done the trick. But the dead slugs would have been eaten by birds and the poison would have been passed on. There had to be an alternative. Fortunately a TV programme that same evening gave the answer – heavily salted water. Drop in the slugs and they die quickly, and nothing goes into the soil.

So, off I go with a bucket of very salty water and start collecting slugs. I stopped when the bucket was full! Next day I did it again. By the end of the week, the neighbours had ceased to be amazed by this mad woman in the garden at night with a torch and a bucket. Because of the numbers, I even started counting as I drowned (yes, complete anorak!). Each evening I was collecting between 400 and 500 slugs.

It was pretty hard work and took most of the spring and early summer to get a balance (the work did reduce to three times a week rather than every night). But the plants grew, no birds were killed and no other creatures were affected. The bird population increased over the following years and they kept the slugs under control for me. A jolly good result all round.

So, to sum up, the basic practice of organic growing revolves around good garden hygiene (more of that in later chapters), working with nature in all its forms and being aware of larger environmental effects.

Food benefits of growing organically

"So, why should we eat organic food?" I hear you ask. "What's in it for us?"

From my personal experience, I can say better general health. Since eating solely organic food, I do feel livelier. I haven't changed what I eat all that much; I've simply bought the same sort of produce but made sure it was organic. Most of the fruit and vegetables I grow myself, anyway.

If I am honest, I have to say that eating organic food has not made me look like a Hollywood starlet; but that was asking rather a lot of it, as I was never tall, slim and devastatingly beautiful! However, I can say that the difference to my appearance is visible. I am no taller, but I am leaner and I have much more energy. Even my eyes look brighter – others have commented on this! Both my husband and I have noticed a definite reduction in colds and other minor ailments.

So why not just buy organic fruit and vegetables from the supermarket? Well, that is a start – a step in the right direction. But I feel that you are missing out on three very important factors – improved freshness, taste, and vitamin content.

It has been found by a number of researchers that all fruit and vegetables begin to lose their vitamin content from the moment they are harvested. This process is natural and inevitable. The rate of loss is steady, so the longer the produce is stored, the more content will be lost.

Even the best supermarket selling organically grown produce will not get it to the customer in less than four days, and usually it is very much longer.

Compare this to the time period involved in lifting or cutting vegetables from your garden/yard/balcony, carrying it to the kitchen, washing and peeling, then cooking. Even if you prepare a meal well in advance, you are talking hours rather than days!
The most obvious benefit, though difficult to quantify, is taste. Defining the taste of a food is quite difficult. Taste is personal and relative, and involves the eyes and nose as well as the mouth. If you have eaten a raw carrot or radish, you will know what they taste like. But this is actually only a trace of the real taste.

Food grown organically takes a little longer to mature than food grown intensively, as it isn't being hustled on by the extra fertilisers. There is more time for the plant to produce the full content of its flavour.

Because there is little travelling time between harvesting and eating when the crop is growing outside your home, the produce is left on the plant until it is fully ripe. Almost all commercial producers, including organic producers who supply supermarkets, pick the crop when it is slightly under-ripe to allow for the travelling and shelf time. So most bought fruit and vegetables are eaten under-ripe, before the full flavour has developed.

You can even see the freshness. Really fresh fruit and vegetables have a sharpness of colour. They are firm to the touch, and skins and pods tend to be much thinner. This freshness is part of the taste factor and does add considerably to the whole experience. This experience you will really enjoy from your own produce.

Personal benefits

On a personal level, you will get a lot of satisfaction from your own produce. There is a definite thrill when you lift a crop of potatoes or see beans forming after the lovely flowers. To know that the crisp lettuce on your plate is a direct result of your own (and nature's) effort is very pleasing. Although I have grown food for more years than I am prepared to admit, I still get a thrill from seeing produce grow, and my family still gets impatient to lift the first fresh potatoes in the spring.

AND, you will know exactly what you are eating. You have been in charge of the process and know that nothing harmful is in the food. What a marvellous piece of information!

We hear a lot these days about the need to take more exercise; there are numerous courses, regimes and classes. So how about this for an exercise programme: instead of touching your toes, bend to plant a seed; don't just stretch your arms into the air, stretch to pick runner beans; gently work your spine hoeing away the weeds; and the lifting of a basket of apples or potatoes will complete your programme. All this in the fresh air and for free. Great isn't it?

Environmental benefits

Embedded in the organic attitude is a respect for the environment, both locally and worldwide.

On a local scale, increasing the natural life and content of your soil encourages and sustains other, larger wildlife. Probably the most noticeable are birds, but you will also encourage frogs, toads, hedgehogs and that best friend of the gardener, earthworms. All these are a genuine help in keeping down pests and adding their share of droppings to the organic content to your soil.

> **One bit of sparrow dropping may not seem much, but if you have a whole family of sparrows living in your garden, they will contribute about a bucketful of manure over a year – all for free and largely put where it can do good.**

Food miles

We hear a lot about "food miles" on the many environmental programmes currently available – that is the distance food has travelled from the producer to the supermarket shelves.

This travel uses fossil fuels (whether in a lorry or plane), creates pollution from exhaust gases and adds considerably to the cost of the food to the consumer.

We used to live in Cornwall (SW England) where the main winter crop is cauliflowers. In season, these are cut, crated and shipped by lorry all over the UK. A large number go to the central warehouses of the major supermarkets. There they are allocated and sent to the various branches. There is a branch of one supermarket chain within five miles of where the vegetables are grown; but the cauliflowers on that shop's shelves have travelled around 350 miles to get there.

You don't have to be a mathematician or scientist to see the nonsense in sending a cauliflower 350 miles, using fuel and man-hours, when it need only travel 5 miles from field to shop!

Recently, another supermarket has been advertising "locally grown" carrots in its branch at Hereford in the Midlands of the UK. This claim is absolutely correct; the carrots are grown on nearby farms. What is not said is that, after picking, the carrots are sent to Peterborough (the other side of the country) to be washed and bagged and then returned to Hereford for sale – round trip of 266 miles (428 kilometres) for "locally grown" produce.

Then, on top of all that, we get into our cars and drive to the shops to buy and bring our food home.

The most economical way to reduce the food miles and the carbon footprint of your food is to produce it organically yourself and keep the travel factor down to a minimum. Although my own growing plot is at the far end of my garden, my produce only travels eighty yards at maximum, and the energy used to transport it is my own. A pretty good use of resources.

Cost benefits

For many families the cost of their food is a considerable factor in their buying habits. It has not helped the commercial growers that it seems more expensive to grow produce organically.

Organic growing does produce a slightly smaller crop which takes slightly longer to reach maturity than would be obtained from liberal use of quick fertilisers and intensive methods. It is also more labour intensive. All these factors create a noticeably higher price in the supermarket. Add the fact that much of commercial farming is heavily subsidised, so what you pay does not accurately reflect the real cost of production.

This is where growing your own produce really pays off. The basic costs are relatively low (seed and the like), the ancillary requirements (manure, compost) are often free and the labour is free – you and your family.

If you were mathematically minded and were to allocate a financial value to your time and effort, you could find a real "cost" of your produce. A recent such exercise has shown that the end cost of home-grown organic produce is considerably less than bought organic food and almost the same as the massed-produced varieties. (If you offset the cost of going to the gym against the work on your produce, it comes down even more!)

If you have to use containers and bought compost initially, this will be a one-off expense. In subsequent years, you will re-use the containers and make your own compost.

Real savings can be made on more expensive items such as seasonal fruits. After the initial expense of buying a fruit tree, the costs get less every year of the tree's life. Bearing in mind that a fruit tree can live for twenty productive years or more, you can have saved lots from each tree you plant. Even a few strawberry plants will last five to six years. Getting the message?

So, now you are ready to begin. Let's look at what you have and what you are going to do with it.

DOWN TO EARTH

CHAPTER THREE

Beat the Jargon

CHAPTER

THREE

As you read your seed packets, magazines, websites and gardening books, you will come across items you do not fully understand. This is not unusual – all activities attract their own jargon.

Gardeners, particularly long-term gardeners, understand these technical terms, and so assume that everyone does. This may not be the case. So to help out, here are some of the more common bits of jargon, with, we hope, a reasonable explanation. It is not a definitive list, so we would like to hear from you about any others you have come across.

Annuals/bi-annuals/perennials

As seen on seed packets, this refers to the growing cycle of the plant. *Annuals* will grow, flower and fruit in one year (most vegetables). *Bi-annuals* take two years to reach maturity and produce fruits (e.g. figs in cooler climates or onions grown from seed). *Perennials* grow and crop every year (e.g. fruit trees and bushes, grape vines, rhubarb). Note that a fruit tree may not fruit the year you plant it because of this disturbance, or it simply may be too young.

Biological controls

Even an organic garden sometimes needs some help with pest control. The trend is to introduce natural predators to devour the pests. Good practices will encourage natural allies – toads, ladybirds (ladybugs), hoverflies, lacewings, hedgehogs, and so forth. Alternatively, you can introduce other predators. The most common are nematodes, put on the soil to help protect against slugs and snails or vine weevil, and *Encarsia* wasps, to defend against whitefly. All are available commercially.

Blanching

Some vegetables (e.g. leeks and celery) are preferred with long white stems, rather than green. This is produced by excluding the light from the stems during growth, either by "earthing up" (see entry later in this chapter) or by covering the stems with a collar (tube) of dark plastic or paper, leaving the tops free. The collar will need to be loosened as the plant grows, but will exclude the light effectively.

Bolting

Unnaturally fast growth resulting in the early production of flowers and seeds is known as bolting. This is usually caused by either a sudden cold spell when the plant is young or excessively dry soil. The plant responds by making seed as quickly as possible to offset the threat. The result for the grower is no crop. It is usually found in *Brassica*s and onions. To avoid, choose cultivars that are bolt-resistant or plant out when conditions are more favourable. There is no way of altering the plant once it has happened. Also known as *going to seed*.

Cloche

A relatively small cover used for the protection of plants against pests or cold. They can be sufficient to cover a single plant and are usually round (recycle note: a litre soft drink bottle with the bottom cut off makes an ideal cloche for individual young plants). They can also be a long, low tunnel made of hoops covered with plastic to cover a row of plants or prevent frost reaching the ground and so heating it up earlier.

Catch crop

A second crop planted with or by a first, to use the ground. The second crop is slower growing and will complete its growth after the first is finished. For example, sow parsnip and radish together; pick the radish and leave the parsnip to mature (this also saves a lot of thinning out; see later in list).

Chitting

Starting off seed potatoes before planting them into their growing space, by laying them in a tray in the light until healthy small sprouts grow from the "eyes" (the spots on the surface of the tuber).

Cold frame

A cold frame is a simple, unheated container for plants with a glass top and solid sides. It is usually built at ground level and is much smaller than a greenhouse, although it does a similar job. The sides can be built from wood, brick or block, and the glass top should be able to be opened and stay propped open as necessary. It is possible to buy ready-made frames, but they are easily built from materials to hand – an old window is an ideal top. Cold frames do not need to be in direct sunlight but should not be in deep shade either.

Companion planting

Growing plants together to help each other (e.g. onions next to carrots; nasturtiums with cucumbers or similar; runner beans and sweet corn). Believed to help deter predators.

Compost/manure

In general, a compost is a form of nutritious soil for growing plants in. It can be home-made or bought commercially. (The home-made is recommended for organic growers, as it has been shown to be freer of disease). All composts contain nutrients to help plants grow.

Also *potting compost*: a commercially produced soil used specifically for raising seeds and young plants. It is usually a very fine texture with controlled nutrient levels and sterilised to reduce disease. Always choose registered organic commercial composts and then add to your garden or compost maker after use.

Crop rotation

The planning of a growing space to ensure that crops are grown in a different area each year. This prevents the build-up of crop-specific diseases and the depletion of the soil by greedy plants. In containers, different crops should be grown or the soil content changed totally if using for the same type of crop.

Cross pollination

The fertilising of the flowers of one plant by the pollen from another is usually carried out naturally by garden insects. This is particularly necessary for many fruit trees and bushes, where two trees need to be planted to pollinate each other. Increasingly, recent fruit tree types are being bred that are "self fertile" and can be planted alone, but will still produce fruit.

Crown

The top of a plant where the stalks or branches grow from. Particularly used for trees (the whole collection of branches) and rhubarb (the base of the plant).

Cultivar

The specific, named variety of a crop. They usually have particularly characteristics or habits to suit different areas. For example, the species is "apple", and the cultivar is "Worcester Permain" – hardy, reliable cropping, mildew resistant.

"Cut and come again" crops

Instead of harvesting the entire plant, these crops can be harvested by cutting out the centre and leaving the rest to continue growing and providing a second or more crop. Examples: some lettuces, cabbages, chard or kale.

Dibber

A tool to make a single hole for planting. These can be bought and are usually about 12"/30 cm long, with a bluntly rounded end. You can make one out of a length of broom handle or thick piece of doweling. They are very useful when planting out reasonable sized crops such as cabbage.

Drainage

The rate at which water soaks through soil. Good drainage moves the water through the soil; poor drainage holds it in the upper layers. This keeps it round the roots of your crops, makes them cold and may kill them (it will certainly slow down their growth). Too fast drainage (usually in light soils) means the water passes the plant roots, taking the nutrients with it, without giving them time to benefit. Obviously, a middle way of reasonable drainage is to be aimed for using lots of organic matter (see later in this chapter) in the soil and ensuring the earth is not compacted or solid (and getting waterlogged).

Earthing up

Piling soil against the stem of plants, usually for protection or to encourage growth. This is used particularly with potatoes, as the tubers form towards the end of the roots, so more earth will encourage more roots and more tubers. It also prevents the tubers pushing through into the light. Earthing up is usually done two or three times during the growth period and the soil is piled to leave the top few leaves still showing. (In containers, leave a good space when planting and earth up by adding soil to build up the contents. With leeks and celery, it excludes the light and produces a whiter vegetable.

Fine tilth

The soil which every grower aspires to achieve. It is rich without being heavy, full of nutrients but of a fine, crumbly texture which digs and rakes very easily. Also known as a *fine loam*.

Fertiliser/manure

Any substance which is added to soil or plants to provide food and help them grow. Fertilisers have become known as any semi-concentrated substance in powder, granule or liquid form. Organic fertilisers are produced from plant or animal sources and processed to make them easier to use. Manure is usually considered to be bulkier and nearer the animal or vegetable source – it is rotted compost from the compost heap or the remains and droppings of animals (or a mixture of both). Organic fertilisers and manure are generally slightly slower acting and so ensure steady growth of the plant.

Forcing

To achieve a much earlier crop then you would get naturally, a few plants can be made to grow quicker. This can be done with rhubarb, endive, seakale, chicory and chard. They are grown inside boxes, forcing jars (if you can get them), upturned buckets, boxes or large flowerpots (cover the drainage hole). These exclude the light and keep the area inside a little warmer. They will enable the plants to be ready to cut about three weeks earlier than usual.

Forking

1. Digging over the ground using a fork rather than a spade.

2. What happens to carrots when grown on heavy or stoney ground. The root of the carrot meets a stone and splits to go round it, producing two or more thinner roots rather than one good one.

Foliar feeding

Applying food to a plant through the leaves rather than the roots. This is a good way to boost growth and easy to apply – simply water with a can, giving each plant a good soaking. You can produce home-made feed by soaking comfrey or seaweed in a tub for about two weeks (it is smelly) and then straining, diluting (at least three parts water to one part feed) and applying.

Grafting

A technique for growing one plant on the stem of another. It is particularly used in roses and fruit trees. The basic technique is to attach a twig or bud from one tree (the scion) and fasten it to the root stock of another to produce specific characteristics in the resultant new tree. It is relatively complex and skilled, so probably best left to the professionals, although keen growers may like to try it, particularly if they wish to preserve a rare or unusual tree. Most commercially produced fruit trees and roses are grown from grafted plants, and the supplier should give all the information on this.

Hardening off

When seeds have been planted and started in a greenhouse or on a window ledge, they will be used to a certain temperature. To take them from that temperature to the colder outdoors is not a good idea and, worst case, can kill the young plants. They should instead be introduced gradually to the lower temperatures. Firstly, once there is no chance of frost, take the seed tray/pot outside each morning, but bring it back in before dusk. Do this for about two weeks, gradually increasing the time they are outside. Then, leave them out all the time, but in a warm area protected from too much wind. After about another two weeks, they should be ready to put into the ground or their growing container.

If you have space, build a cold frame (see above). Then place the seedlings in it and open the lid during the day, gradually increasing the time it is open. After about three weeks, they should be ready for planting out.

Humus

Usually considered the organic part of soil, it is actually a complex mix of organisms, rotted substances and compounds. It helps the soil to retain water and nutrients and gives body to its structure.

Long tom pots

These are standard diameter pots, but with much longer bodies. Used for plants which require a deeper root space (e.g. roses). A standard 6"/15 cm pot will be about 6"/15 cm deep; a long tom will be 10"/25 cm deep.

Microclimate

This is an area which has produced a somewhat different set of growing conditions from the larger area around it. The easiest example is a greenhouse, which can simulate the tropics, even when the garden is springtime in the north. In any garden there can be microclimates (e.g. a sunny corner surrounded by walls can be much warmer than the rest and will grow different crops).

Mulch/top dressing

These terms are often considered interchangeable. They do mean the same to a point, in that both refer to something which is put on the surface of the ground. The difference is in the implied reason for putting them on. As a rule of thumb, top dressing implies a substance which is put on the soil with the intention of improving or feeding it (e.g. fertiliser, manure); a mulch is usually put on the soil to protect it, suppress weeds or prevent water loss. It is also usually a thick layer. So, a thick layer of garden compost can be both a mulch and top dressing, but a thick layer of gravel is only a mulch.

Onion sets

The most common way to grow onion sets are baby onions (bulbs) which were grown from seed the previous year. Generally, although more expensive than seed, sets are reliable, easier to grow and less prone to disease.

Organic matter

This is the basis of soil. It is the rotted-down remains of plants which has been taken in to the ground by time, rain and worms. It consists of humus (see above), organisms and nutrients. It is what makes soil brown and gives it its structure. You cannot have too much of it, and it will improve any soil. It does occur naturally when leaves or plants die and fall to the ground or it can be added in the form of garden compost or any manure.

Predators/pests

The gardener usually categorises the insect life in the garden as pests, if they eat the crops, or predators, if they eat the pests. For maximum help to the grower, we need to encourage the predators, to do work for us (see also *biological controls*) whilst minimising the pests.

Pricking out

The process of moving seedlings to a new, larger growing space. After starting seeds in a tray, each one has to be carefully lifted and placed in a small pot to grow individually. This process is necessary for the larger vegetables, such cabbage, sweet corn and tomatoes. Smaller vegetables, such as radishes or carrots, are usually sown straight into the ground and do not like being disturbed (for these see *thinning out*). Pricking out can be tedious, but it is worth the work.

Stopping

To prevent some plants getting too big for their growing space, the growth is stopped by removing the "growing tip" of the plant. This is the name for the end of a branch – often the top of the growing plant. The process is simply to nip or cut off the top part of the stem, which usually has new leaves forming. Stopping can be used to prevent growth or to encourage growth elsewhere, such as from the side shoots (they will take over if the main shoot cannot function).

Strike rate

The percentage of seeds which actually germinate and produce a plant. Most commercially produced seeds have a very high strike rate. If you keep your own seed, it may not have quite so high a rate (but it will be free). Storing seeds for any length of time does reduce the percentage – it is better to use fresh seed each year if you can.

Successional sowing

To give continuity of crops, it is better to sow seeds a little at a time, rather than all at once. Most growers sow seed every two weeks, in slightly smaller quantities, to produce a succession of crops throughout the season.

Thinning out

Vegetables seeds which are sown straight into the space they will grow in may result in plants growing closely together. To allow each plant sufficient growing space, some will need to be removed – this is thinning out. Very young plants will have to be composted as they will not transplant.

Training

Not the gardener – this refers to the growing of fruit trees into a specific shape or to cover a specific area. The most common training is to produce fruit trees to grow up walls and so take up less space. Trees can also be trained along wires or fences. There are a number of basic shapes for training trees – fan, espalier and cordon are the most popular.

True leaves

Each new seedling produces two small leaves very quickly. These are *seed leaves* and the plant can be handled by them during pricking out. Once the plant is growing on, more leaves will be produced, and these are known as true leaves.

Vine

Universally known as the plant grapes grow on. It is also the technical name for the plant which tomatoes grow on. Such tomatoes are harvested as a clump on the stalk, rather than individual fruits. It is believed that they store longer in this form.

Weed

Any plant which is not wanted in the garden. Weeds will take up growing space and, if rampant, will reduce the food available to crops. Many are annuals and easily removed by hoeing, but the pernicious weeds (bramble, dandelion, groundsel, ground elder) should be removed thoroughly or they will take over the entire area.

Yield

The amount of crop produced by a single plant (or packet of seeds if the plants are singles, like carrot). The yield is higher in healthy plants, with more and/or larger fruits. Different cultivars have different yields, so check the seed packet or label for guidance.

CHAPTER FOUR

But I Don't Have a Garden:
How to Use the Space You Do Have

CHAPTER FOUR

What do you have?

The three requirements for growing anything are light, water and soil. So the first thing you must do is look at what space you have now and determine whether it provides these three.

Lack of soil is no real drawback; you can always get some from elsewhere. The other two factors are rather more important, especially light.

So, where are the lighter areas of your garden space? Watch how the sunlight moves – are there areas that get no direct sun, or lots, or some sun for just part of the day? The answers will decide what you grow and where.

Most modern houses seem to have a small plot or paved area attached. This is more than enough to grow a good selection of produce. The average apartment usually has a balcony, and this, too, is adequate – provided it gets light. Where my son lives, it is the custom to erect awnings over the balcony to keep out the sun. He will have to come to an arrangement with his plants and family to share the light.

"But I don't have anything at all!" could be your cry. Now, look really carefully. Do you have a path, flight of steps, wall or doorstep? Do they get some sunlight? You have a growing space!

So let us look at the most common situations:

1. Small patch of soil

In many towns and cities, there are rows of old, terraced houses with a small yard behind, often surrounded by walls. Many modern developments follow a similar pattern, but have fences instead of walls. Somewhere in that enclosed area there is usually a small patch of soil. In my home town, the smallest patch I have seen was 6' x 3' (1.9 m x 1 m), up against a wall.

Many newly built houses have an enclosed patch of bare earth. Most of these are still quite small. If you want somewhere to sit outside and a laundry dryer or clothes line, that takes up about half of the space. On average, you are left with approximately 10' (3 m) square of actual soil.

Both patches, however small, can be enough to feed you, if used fully. You can also extend your "soil" with containers, pots, troughs, gro-bags, etc.

2. Paved yard

Many houses with a very small back garden have, in recent years, been paved over for convenience (particularly by non-gardening owners). This gives the impression that concrete or stone paving slabs is all that you have. But, in fact, nature is lurking underneath, waiting to be let out.

In many cases, the paving slabs have been laid on a thin layer or a few blobs of cement or, best of all, sand. These are the easiest to deal with. They can be lifted relatively easily by the use of a pickaxe and some brute strength.

So, lift up a few slabs, either in a group or in one area, to produce a small growing patch; or dot them around and use each separate area for a different crop. Whichever you choose, do take care to remove the cement as well as the slab – don't be tempted to mix it with the soil underneath; it is not a growing medium and it will change the nature of the soil itself. Sand can be mixed in with the soil for drainage, but you will have to add extra compost to offset the dryness

If, like my elder son's new house, you find you have paving slabs on top of solid cement, on top of other cement, or similar horrors and you don't fancy spending hours (days?) trying to find the soil underneath, then treat your area as follows:

3. No soil at all

A large number of people live in homes with no access to the earth – apartments, condominiums, shared houses, and so forth. Sometimes, if they are lucky, there is some enclosed parking space or an area to hang out laundry (in my younger son's apartment, the laundry area is on the roof).

In these cases, you apply the questions we posed originally. Where is there a patch which gets light? What can you put there? Is it big enough to take a large container or only a small pot? Somewhere, you will find a growing space, even if it only a window ledge or doorstep.

> **Why light is important – a short technical moment.**
> The green colour in plants is due to a pigment called chlorophyll. Chlorophyll combines with sunlight, the carbon dioxide in the air and water from the soil to create a reaction and produce the food which plants need to live (in the form of starch or sugar), with oxygen being expelled as a waste product. This process is called photosynthesis.
> In short – if the plant cannot get light, it cannot make food and it won't grow properly

The most obvious sign of poor light is what growers call "leggy" growth. Here, the plant tries to reach what light there is by growing towards it as quickly as possible. It doesn't bother about growing other parts such as leaves or producing seeds; it just goes hell-for-leather towards the light.

The result is a tall, skinny plant with thin stalks, just like that teenage growth stage when children look to be all legs, hence the name. Sometimes it will lean towards the light as well, particularly if the light comes from one direction only. In fact, these plants often fall over, because the stems are not strong enough to support them.

These are not healthy plants!

There are a few food plants which will grow in poor light, but they are very few. Gooseberry bushes and clumps of rhubarb will tolerate some shade, but these really are the only ones.

But all is not lost! Many plants will cope if they get good light for part of the day and then mediocre light for the rest, such as on an east-facing balcony. The slightly more robust types of vegetables (potatoes, runner beans, carrots) should produce a reasonable crop, even in these conditions.

The majority of fruit trees and shrubs, however, will find it much more difficult. You could well end up with an apple tree with masses of leaves (to produce as much food for the tree as possible) but not one apple for you.

If you are not sure, plant a few salad crops (lettuce, radish, spring onions) in your space and see if they grow "leggy" and feeble. If they do, you will have to look for an alternative site and, perhaps, borrow a bit of land or yard area from a friend.

What about temperature?

a. Too cold

All plants need some warmth to help them grow and ripen. At the very start, seeds need it to nurture the growing process. They will not actually start growing if the ground is too cold. (Remember: lots of water in soil keeps the temperature down. So wet soil is nearly as bad as cold soil.)

Read the seed packet instructions carefully and do not be tempted into sowing too early outdoors. All you will get is frustrated – and rotted seeds.

Another plant enemy is frost. A sudden spring frost will cool young plants so quickly that they cannot grow. A really heavy frost will freeze the sap inside the stems – not good news for a young plant. So do not plant outdoors if there is a risk of frost – wait a few days to be sure.

But at the other end of the growing cycle, there are some plants which do not care about cold, once they are established. Many *Brassica*s (greens) actually carry on growing well into the winter, particularly brussels sprouts and white, coleslaw cabbage. One belief, held widely in northern counties of the UK, is that celery and leeks should not be picked until after the first frost of the autumn, as it makes them taste better (check it out for yourselves).

b. Too hot

Knowing that plants needs warmth to grow, can it be too hot? The answer is both no and yes!

Many fruit trees and plants actually love the heat, as it ripens the fruit. Strawberries, for example, need the warmth to produce more sugar so we get large, sweet fruits. Tomatoes, peppers and chillies do too. In many northern areas, these can only be grown in greenhouses, although milder areas grow them outdoors quite easily. In most cases, however, it is the heat they need, not necessarily actual sunlight (tomatoes, certainly, prefer to be warm, but out of direct light).

This where the "no" factor kicks. Sometimes it is too hot and the plants can die of thirst, because the water evaporates off before they have had the benefit of it. I have noticed that in some Mediterranean countries, salad and similar plants are grown inside poly-tunnels covered in very thick, semi-opaque plastic. This diffuses the sunlight and slows down the water loss without cutting out the light.

A system anyone can use is to cover the surface of your growing area with a really thick mulch (see chapter 3) of shredded bark, fine gravel or home-made compost. All these will slow down evaporation of water from the soil.

Alternately, only grow crops which suit your conditions.

Seasonal plants

Supermarkets have spoiled us with their wide variety of fruit and vegetables, shipped (flown) in, from all over the world. We have become used to eating strawberries or green peas whenever we like, rather than when they are in season. The price we pay for this choice, of course, is a considerable reduction in taste and nutritional value. [Personally, I feel that the snob value of serving tasteless strawberries at Christmas is greatly over-rated – daft, in fact.]

One adjustment you will have to make is to accept that you will only have certain crops at certain times of year. You will be able to store your crops, if you produced more than you need to eat fresh, and this will still be better than non-organic food. But the real bonus is that glorious taste of food in season

One word of caution – some crops cannot be grown in some areas, even in season. For instance, in cooler areas, you can grow runner beans but, possibly, not French beans (they need a bit more warmth). In warmer, more tropical, areas, the opposite might be true.

So, unless you have enough space and facilities for glasshouses and specialist growing conditions, plan your plot with your local climate and the seasons in mind.

4. Window ledge

Probably the smallest available light area anyone will have is a window ledge. In a modern home, this is likely to be inside only and about 1.5 m/5' long by 15 cm/6" wide (more if you are lucky). In an older property, there could be an outside window ledge, too.

At first glance, this does not seem like a lot of space for growing, but it doesn't mean you can grow nothing.

The most obvious small items for the window ledge are herbs. Most herbs do not need a big pot to grow in. Many, particularly the Mediterranean herbs (basil, marjoram, sage, thyme), actually grow better if the soil is limited. (Think of the hot, dry Mediterranean hillside, which is what their natural growing conditions are like.) Using a smallish pot, say 6"/15 cm across the top, you can grow three different fresh herbs to add to your cooking.

During the summer, on an outside window ledge, and all year round indoors, grow salad. Yes, you can! Two 6"/15 cm pots, each with a cut and come again lettuce in it, plus one pot of radishes and one of spring onions, and you are set. You can get continuous crops (posh words: successional sowing) by starting a second crop in a spare pot, two weeks later and replacing the window ledge as you use them.

On an outdoor window ledge, try a few leeks in a tallish pot, say, three plants to a 9"/22 cm "long tom" pot (see chapter 3), or two plants of purple sprouting broccoli, through the winter. Your main problem could be the wind, so be sure to anchor the pots or window box firmly.

A more recent trend, although much used by vegetarians for many years, is the growing of sprouts in a glass jar. This is not brussels sprouts, but newly germinated seeds, such as beans or peas. You have probably used bean sprouts in Chinese cookery.

Method: half fill a large jar with pea, chickpea, haricot bean, radish, mung bean, alfalfa seeds, or similar. Add a very little water, shake gently and watch them grow. When the sprouts are about ½"/1 cm long, drain and add to your next stir-fry.

Alternatively, spread a thin layer of seeds on a sheet of damp blotting paper. Keep the paper damp and monitor as above. Provided you can ensure that light can get to each level, you can stack your growing levels and increase your crops

How's that for starters?

5. Basement Area

Now let's look at probably the most troublesome growing space – the (usually) smallish patch in front of a basement flat/apartment. It is often surrounded by high walls, up to the street/ground level and may have steps taking up part of the space.
Whichever way the building faces, any light which reaches this space is coming from high up, and any direct sunlight probably won't last long.

On the face of it, this is not a convenient growing area. But let's look a little closer. Which way does the house face? If it's southeast, south or southwest, you have an upright, sunny growing area. A northerly view will need a bit more help, but it should mean that the steps or opposite wall is south facing.

Unless you are very fortunate, the ground level may not be very light. So start there to encourage more light into your area. Surface your flat ground with a light coloured cover– pale sandstone paving or cobbles; cream gravel; if cement, paint with light-coloured masonry or cement paint.

Now lighten the walls. Paint is the easiest and cheapest way to do this. Again, choose a light colour. It doesn't have to be stark white; light blue, palest grey, buttercup yellow and pale green will all work just as well and look pretty at the same time. So you have maximised the light, now maximise the growing space – go upwards!

A simple ploy is to put some trellis, netting or wires up a piece of wall for runner beans to climb up. A friend of mine, Norman, lives in a ground-floor flat and uses the side of a spiral staircase going to the flat above. He runs strings from the bars of the staircase to canes in the growing bed, and up the beans go. He can pick the beans by simply walking up the steps. He can leave this arrangement in place permanently, as runner beans are the one crop you can grow in the same place on successive years (see *crop rotation*, chapter 3).

Alternately, fix wall baskets, troughs or hay racks to the wall at regular intervals and plant each with a different crop. Use window ledges for boxes, and suspend hanging baskets as high as you can sensibly reach.

6. Balconies

The need for more housing is resulting in more of us living in apartment blocks and condominiums. Parking spaces are probably the only open area such locations have. Fortunately, most also have a balcony. If you are lucky, it is a large, sunny balcony, but any size is enough to grow in.

Balconies usually provide light, fresh air, sometimes rain, and a flat surface which will take some weight. On the downside, they may be windy, which will add to the drying factor (more of this under *watering later in this chapter*).

Most people with balconies have a few plants on them. So, instead of ornamental plants, why not grow something useful and healthy?

All growing on a balcony will be in some form of container. These can range from plastic utilitarian plant pots, through ornamental pots and troughs, to large elegant planters if you have the space (and money).

All containers need some drainage or they will get waterlogged, so bear in mind that the water will need to run somewhere – off the balcony rather than into the apartment.

If, like my younger son, you live in a hot country, it may be the custom to cover all balconies with awnings to keep most of the sunlight out. In these cases, you may have to make an arrangement with the human resident to close the awning for some period of each day to let the plants have the light

7. Steps and stairs

An often-ignored area, outside steps and stairs can be a useful growing space.

The simplest system is a medium-sized pot on each step, with a different crop or herb in each. This is a really simple way to grow salad and smaller vegetables such as carrot or parsnip and almost any herb, especially the culinary ones – parsley, thyme, sage, mint, basil, oregano – all the lower-growing varieties.

Generally speaking, these will need very little attention, as they are open to rain and light naturally. Like everything container-grown, they may have to be watered in dry weather.

Remember, also, that steps have an outside, as well as an inside. This might be a wall to which you can fasten wall pots or hanging baskets. It may have a handrail and upright supports which will guide a climbing plant or fasten a pot holder. Sometimes the end of the step protrudes beyond the railings; this is another resting place for a pot.

Check out your steps for light and then use your imagination.

8. Containers

Many homes have no open soil available, so growing in containers is a necessity. This necessity does not have to be boring or ugly. There are lots of ornamental and fashionable containers available to suit your decor, property or tastes.

What are the advantages of using containers?

Suit your area. You can choose style, size, even colour, to produce the effect you want or to fit in with a small or oddly shaped space. Even the most luxurious penthouse can have elegant, fashionable containers, and the food crops, shrubs or trees will not look out of place.

Pots and containers can be moved around. This might be a distinct advantage if you have limited light. You can move the pots to give each crop a share of the sun. But do remember to put larger containers on wheels or you will injure yourself doing this (which is not part of our plan).

You can grow a variety of crops – one to each container. Young plants can be started on your window ledge and then planted out into a pot outside to give continuation of crops. Larger containers allow for mixed and companion planting (see chapter 5), which can be ornamental as well as useful.

You have good control or the soil. Because a container has only one type of plant in it, the soil/compost you use can be tailored to that crop's needs. So, greens can have heavy, rich soil in their container, whilst herbs will get light, drier soil. It is also easier to avoid problems and diseases by using a container for a completely different crop once the first crop has been harvested.

9. Going up the wall

In a number of cities, notably Paris, there has been a recent trend towards growing vertically, if ground space is scarce. This is quite a sensible idea, as it gives the plants access to air and light and raises them above potential damage.

The only real problem with vertical growing is water and food. The owners of the buildings where this method has been developed use a complex support structure and hydroponic feeding – putting nutrients into water and dribbling it across the plant roots through a series of fine pipes. It works very well, but is very expensive to run and uses a considerable amount of power for pumps and water recycling, so is not organic (the nutrients have to be artificial to be easily assimilated into the water).

For a domestic area, perhaps we can achieve the same effect more simply.

One choice is to grow plants which climb naturally. Possible choices are grape vines or kiwi fruit (if you are looking to brew your own beer, you may try hops, as well). Both will happily go up a wall, with a bit of support. Fix some trellis, strings or wires to the wall and catch in the plant as it grows.
BUT both of these need warmth, particularly the kiwi fruit. If your wall catches plenty of sun, they will probably survive happily. If you have cooler conditions or cold winters, you will have to cover the plants warmly through the cold times.

A number of fruit trees will adapt to growing against a wall, and benefit from the extra warmth it can hold. They will need a good piece of earth or a deep container, wires or trellis to support them, and gentle pruning to keep them flat against the wall as they grow. The R.H.S. website *(www.rhs.org.uk)*

has excellent pages on pruning fruit trees, which guide you, step-by-step. The easiest shape is probably a fan, but see what suits your area.

Then there are the annual vegetables – peas and beans. Runner beans (stick beans, climbing beans, string beans) need to climb and will happily reach 8'/2½ m or more, if allowed to. French/dwarf beans and peas are less frantic and will only need 3–4"/1–1½ m depending on which type you choose.

If none of these options tempts you, then hang wall pots and plant as suggested previously (remember the watering and some feeding).

What goes up can also come down

Thinking vertically – a long plant can hang down as easily as climb up. So your climbing beans can be planted at the top of a flight of steps and you can pick them as they grow downwards towards you.

But the real champions for growing downwards have to be strawberries. You can plant them in a window box or hanging basket and they will cascade naturally. The added advantage, particularly with hanging baskets, is that it is much harder for the slugs and snails to get at your fruit. You can see them clearly if they are mountaineering up the wall and dispose of them before they do damage.

An average hanging basket (wire or plastic) is about 12"/30 cm diameter and this will take three or four plants. An ornamental terra cotta wall pot will take a single plant. Watering is essential, as with all containers, but there is little else to do except pick the fruit.

It is also easy to grow tomatoes in a hanging basket. Most types will adapt although some robust types could be very heavy due to the considerable crop. The easiest is "Tumbler", which, as the name suggests, was developed for hanging containers. Otherwise, choose lightish outdoor types such as "Outdoor Girl" or "Gardener's Delight" (a cherry tomato).

Hanging baskets are particularly useful in a basement area, as they bring the crop nearer the light.

As with individual pots, you can use a small basket (say 6"/15 cm diameter) for single type of plant. In a standard basket, you can mix your crops. A tomato plant could be surrounded by parsley or radish. A ring of strawberry plants can have a lettuce or two in the middle of them (say, Tom Thumb).

Even if you are growing on a window ledge, you can hang a pot from above the window a swell and double your growing area.

Give yourself more growing time

However large or small space we have, we all want to get the most out of it. So, if we can't increase the space, let's look at how we can increase the growing time we have available.

How to avoid the winter cold? Obviously, some plants will grow outdoors in the colder months, so some space can be given to them. Hardiest are the greens (*Brassica*s), particularly brussels sprouts, cabbages, kale and leeks. There are also a few winter lettuces and radishes.

One of the easiest ways to prolong growing is in a greenhouse. Even without heat, some hardy salads and vegetables (e.g. winter carrots) will continue to grow through the year. But the real advantage of a greenhouse is for starting your planting and growing early. You can plant seed and raise them to small plants weeks before you could outdoors. Some plants can stay in the greenhouse and be picked earlier, or the young plants can be planted out when the soil outside warms up, and will carry on growing and be mature earlier.

One good side effect is that more-mature plants are less likely to be attacked by predators or diseases (with the exception of rabbits or next-door's cat), giving you a better yield. Also the birds will not eat young plants or dig up the seeds.

If space is limited, there are "mini" greenhouses on the market. These are usually about 5"/1½ m high, 2"/60 cm wide and covered in polythene. Put in a sheltered part of your patch (not necessarily on soil), they can house all your seedlings till planting time. If you are practical yourself, you can build a frame over part of your space and cover with plastic sheeting or corrugated plastic, to give the same facility.

Water, water!

Regularly in this chapter, I have harped on about watering. As we defined originally, water is an essential part of photosynthesis and, therefore, healthy plant growth. Don't get too paranoid about it, but do watch for the signs.

If a plant is thirsty, it will droop. The leaves will hang down limply and the stems will start to curve. So water at once. If it gets too bad, the leaves will begin to go yellow or brown, like in autumn. This could be more serious, but water anyway. You will know within twenty-four hours if it will survive – it will have lifted and will be looking greener.

Sometimes, in our eagerness, we can overwater. Unfortunately, the symptoms are very similar to underwatering. So first check the soil. Stick a finger into the soil and feel what it's like. If it's damp and cool, it has enough water, so leave well alone.

If you are growing in containers, you should have provided plenty of drainage material in the bottom of the pot, under the soil. This should be adequate to prevent the pot getting waterlogged. If it does seems waterlogged, because you are in a wet area or the weather is particularly bad, raise the pot off the ground on stones or pot feet. If this still does not produce an improvement, you may have to completely repot the plants in fresh, dryer compost and check the drainage in the container.

All other conditions being equal, watering containers once a day if it doesn't rain, and open ground daily during drought, should be enough.

> Allotment tip:
> A reasonable amount of regularly is better than masses of once and then nothing for ages. Also, a little bit is no good at all – at least half a watering can for a good-sized container (2' or more diameter).

> Green practice.
> Wherever possible, use natural water, without chemicals. So, save all the water you can, by collecting from roofs into water butts/tanks or even putting buckets outside when it rains. You can even save washing-up water to put on your plants (they don't mind soap at all).

How much can I grow?

Everything needs enough space to grow in. If crops are crowded, you may get abnormal growth (some tall and leggy, others stunted) and you won't get a good yield. So how much actual growing space will you need?

Containers

1. An 8″/20 cm diameter x 7½″/19 cm high pot will grow any of the following:
    - A light sprinkling of carrot seed (thinned out to about twelve adult carrots)
    - Four "Little Gem" lettuces or two standard lettuces (say "Lollo Rosso")
    - Twenty radishes
    - Three good-sized parsnips
    - One seed potato, producing about ¾ kg/1½ lbs eatable potatoes
    - One tomato plant
    - One pepper or chilli plant
    - One small bay tree or herb bush (e.g. marjoram, rosemary)

So, choose from the list what you want to grow, and buy enough plastic pots (one for each crop), and you have the basis of a kitchen garden.

2. A larger, 10″/25 cm diameter, 10½″/27 cm high pot will hold the following:
    - 25 per cent more of the above
    - Two runner bean plants on sticks

- Four leeks
- One large coleslaw or savoy cabbage
- One kale or spinach plant (more leaves will grow as you cut it)
- One courgette plant (about six actual courgettes)

3. A large, ornamental container, say 15"/38 cm diameter, 13"/33 cm high will hold the following:
   - Four runner bean plants on poles
   - Two tomato vines
   - Eight sweetcorn
   - One fruit tree – apple, pear, plum or peach/nectarine (in warmer areas)
   - One grapevine.

Even a little 3"/7½ cm pot will grow some radishes or a small lettuce on the window ledge.

If you have a patch of soil, it is estimated that you can grow enough food to feed two people on an area 10'/3½ m square. This will grow beans, peas, carrots, beetroot and salad through the summer and alternate with cabbage, kale and leeks through the winter. The R.H.S. at Harlow Carr has been researching the capacity of a small plot. Results and advice can be obtained through their website.

Now you have seen what you have and need to decide what to do with it. So, on to the next stage.

CHAPTER FIVE

Getting Started

CHAPTER FIVE

So, you've assessed your space and worked out where you are going to grow your crops. You've decide how you are going to grow them and the containers or areas they will be in. You've decided what actual crops you will grow and how many of them.

Then let's begin with the actual work you need to do now.

Tools and equipment

Whatever your growing space, you will need a few basic tools. Unless you really want to, or have generous present-givers around, you do not have to stock up with every modern gardening gadget. Keep it simple.

A basic necessity is a good trowel. It should be a convenient size and weight to suit your hand grip and physical strength. The only recommendation I would make is that it be metal rather than plastic. Metal will last longer and work the soil easier, because the blade of the trowel is thinner. Also, whilst you don't want tools that are so heavy you can hardly lift them, choose one which is the heaviest you can cope with. A combination of weight and gravity makes the trowel more efficient at going through the soil, so your work will be easier.

If you are growing entirely in containers, a trowel is really all you need. If you have any sort of patch of land, however, you will also need a spade, a rake and, possibly, a fork.

When buying a spade, hold it as if you were lifting soil; imagine the blade full of wet earth. Could you still lift it? Then you've found the right weight and size for you.

> Tip:
> the blade of the spade should be moderately narrow with a new sharp front edge to go through soil easily.

It is often easier to dig over heavier soils, at first, with a fork. This is particularly true with clay soils (see later in this chapter) or where the ground has been compacted. Compacted soil is earth which has been pressed down over the years until it forms a solid lump. This is usually because it has had something on top such as a shed, pathway or lawn. But if your soil is fairly loose or soft, you can dig it with a spade.

Either way, you will still need to rake it level afterwards.

Pots and containers

If growing in containers, this is where the decision is made. How big and what sort?

It doesn't matter to the plants whether the pot is coloured, decorative or fashionable, just so long as it has room to grow. So, choose the style and appearance of your containers to suit yourself and your space. Simply make sure it is big enough and has drainage holes at the bottom (plastic containers can be drilled to give drainage holes, but ceramic are much trickier, so buy them ready done).

If you are planning to put containers in one place and not move them, then go for as big as you like. On the other hand, if you may want to move them around in the future and you can only just lift the container when it's empty, you will have real problems when it's full of compost. Think ahead – think possibly wheels underneath.

General equipment

You may need some smaller items to help you grow seeds up to the planting out stage. Much of this can be recycled items (see next section). The basics are as follows:

- Seed tray. Shallow (1½"/4 cm) tray or bowl, with drainage holes in the bottom, for sowing seed into. They are made in various sizes, depending how many seeds you want to grow in them.

- Shallow pots and half-pots. Some larger seeds, such as peas or beans, can be started off in small pots (about 2½"/6 cm diameter). This will give them a bit more depth of soil than a seed tray. Larger quantities can be sown in a "half-pot" which is approximately 6"/15 cm in diameter but only about 4"/10 cm deep (it saves on compost and doesn't get as cold as a full depth pot).

- Watering can. Any size, but fitted with a fine "rose" nozzle

- Seedling lifter for "pricking out" seedlings (see chapter 3), from seed tray to larger pot for growing on. You can buy these, but a plastic label, spoon handle or old, small knife blade will do just as well.

- Labels. Anything which will stick into a seed tray or pot, with the plant name clearly written on it. Very necessary if you are not sure what the young plants look like, or you can't remember what you planted.

As much of the organic ethos is strongly against waste, recycling is practised wherever possible. So let's see what you can get for nothing (or very little) to use on your plot.

Recycled equipment

1. The yoghurt pot/tub

A standard 125g yoghurt pot makes an ideal plant pot. With a couple of holes in the bottom, it will take a larger seed (tomato, courgette, pea, bean) up to planting out size.

A bigger pot is just about the same size as a 6"/15 cm half-pot and can be used to start off seeds in the same way (lettuce, parsnip).

If you are protecting crops by covering with netting draped over canes, a pot on the top of each cane gives support, stops the netting slipping over and prevents the cane poking you.

2. The cake tray

Supermarkets often sell small cakes or tray bakes, in shallow plastic or foil trays. These make ideal seed trays, particularly if you only wish to plant a few.

3. Wooden fruit boxes/cardboard cartons

Shallow boxes or cartons, such as those for tomatoes (single layer) are good for storing your harvest. Fruit and vegetables can be laid in the box, which, in turn can be stacked in your storage area, leaving air space between each layer naturally.

Deeper boxes and crates, such as those for apples and pears, often come with shaped sheets between the layers of fruit. Ask your local store for these and stack your crop like the commercial growers.

Deeper wooden crates also make a serviceable planter. Raise the box a little way off the ground to prevent the base rotting with damp, line with plastic (old compost bags are ideal) and punch some holes or slits in the bottom. Then fill with soil and grow whatever you like – they are deep enough to take any vegetable. If you want decorative, simply paint them to suit (this will protect the box as well).

4. Plastic sacks

Instead of buying prepared "Gro Bags", you can make your own from plastic sacks. The more robust kind are the best – those which held potting compost, fertiliser, bulk pet or animal food, sand, cement or gravel.

Usually they already have holes in them; if not just punch a few around the bottom. Then fold the sides down to about half way (do not cut off, the folds will make it more robust), fill with compost/soil and plant up. They, too, will take almost any vegetable.

If you have lots of sacks, use them to cover the soil through the winter to suppress weeds and warm up the soil for earlier sowing.

5. Buckets

A standard plastic bucket (6 pts/15 l) is the growing equivalent of a 12"/30 cm plant pot and is usually much cheaper. They are ideal for growing potatoes (one seed potato per bucket) or beans (three plants). They will last for years and are easy to move around. (Holes in the bottom, as always.)

6. 1 or 2 litre plastic drinks bottles/milk bottles

These are most useful and adaptable. Some suggestions on their use are as follows:

- Cloches: cut off the bottom of the bottle and place one over each new pea, bean, cabbage or courgette plant when you put them out into their growing place, pressing them into the soil. By the time the plant is nearly filling the bottle, it will be strong enough to cope with the pests and the bottle can be removed.
- Scoop: cut off the bottom of a milk bottle (any size) and about half the length of the body to half way up to make a serviceable scoop for compost.
- Bird/cat scarer: fill a clear bottle with water and place on the soil, where it can catch the light. The reflection is supposed to put creatures off (it does work with birds, but I found our local cats soon got used to them).

7. Envelopes

Begin saving envelopes from summer onwards to hold the seeds you will be saving from your own crops. You will need solid envelopes, not ones with a window. Paper envelopes or bags are much better for storage than plastic, as they do not produce condensation, which makes the seeds damp and, therefore, rot. If you have any risk from mice or you are not sure of your storage area, keep the envelopes in a lidded biscuit tin or large (1 litre) ice cream carton.

If you approach your growing with recycling in mind, you will find all sorts of uses for items you would otherwise throw away. Be inventive – all recycling is helpful to the environment!

Deep down and dirty

Having gotten together all you need to start, you now need to check on that vital part of growing – the soil.

Any patch of ground you intend to work needs to be able to sustain the plants you put into it. So, first, look at what you've got to start with.

Soil is generally divided into four categories: heavy clay, sand, chalk, and rich loam. In practice, nature being erratic and inconsiderate, you can have any number of combinations in an area, even within one garden. So long as you can recognise what you've got, you can deal with it.

1. Chalk

This is the easiest type to recognise. The soil at the top is probably light in colour, soft and fine in texture, with bits of white chalk in it and it does not get waterlogged. If you dig a hole, you will probably not go down very far before your spade scrapes on the white, solid chalk layer underneath.

On the plus side, chalk is usually fairly fertile and drains well.

On the minus side, the good drainage takes nutrients away quickly; the bits of chalk or flint in the topsoil can make it very stony and it will have a high lime content, which does not suit a lot of plants.

Chalky soil can be easily helped by adding lots of organic matter, such as farmyard manure or well-rotted garden compost. The drainage issue will always be with you, but you can persuade the topsoil to hold more food and water with more organic matter.

Stoniness can be a problem with carrots and parsnips (see chapter 9), but most other crops will cope.

2. Clay

If you have seen or handled pottery clay, you will know the texture of this type of soil. It is damp, sticky and cold and can be squeezed into different shapes. In the garden, it can stick together in big clods which are very heavy to lift. Really heavy clay soils get sodden in the winter and baked solid in the summer and take ages to warm up in the spring.

Sounds dreadful, doesn't it? But, in fact, clay soil holds a lot of nutrients and some of the bigger plants, such as fruit trees (especially black, red and white currants) and *Brassica*s (cabbage, brussels sprouts) really appreciate it.

Initially you may have to dig it over to loosen up the soil a bit and let some air in. If you can do this in the autumn, you need only dig roughly and leave it for the frost to break it up further (If you live in a frost-free area, sorry, you'll have to dig). A handful of sand or grit dug in with each spadeful will help open up the soil, and with plenty of bulky manure and compost added regularly, it will become easier to work with time and will give good growing results.

3. Sand

As the name suggests, this is a lightweight, paler brown, soft soil. It is easily washed away by heavy rain, particularly on slopes, and water and nutrients drain through it very quickly. Some plants will not be able to get a good root hold, so may not give as good a result as on other soils (brussels sprouts are particularly vulnerable; see chapter 10).

But it is very easy to work: digging is light and weeding is easy. It warms up very quickly in the spring and can often be planted much earlier.

As always, the answer is lots of manure and compost to help retain the water and food and provide good anchorage for the roots.
Silt is a cross between clay and sandy soils. It is the result of deposits by rivers in the past. Although it may compact like clay (so add organic matter), it is usually easy to work and very, very fertile (think of the Nile in Egypt).

4. Rich loam

This soil description actually covers a number of combinations of all of the above. But it always has a rich brown (or reddish-brown) colour; a fresh, earthy smell; a slight dampness without being cold or too sticky; and, although you can't see it by eye, a high nutrient content.

Loam is what every grower aims for – the ideal growing medium. If you are blessed with such soil, rejoice. If not keep working your ground and adding to it and loam will result, eventually.

Remember: even the best soil will lose nutrients to the plants, so still add compost to keep it really healthy (it just won't need quite as much as the other types).

Let's hear it for the earthworm

A good basic test of soil is how many worms there are. Earthworms like a balanced soil that is not too wet and has plenty of food in it. So, check your soil for worms. The more you add to it, the more earthworms you should get.

In a previous garden, we inherited heavy clay which had been neglected and not worked for many years – and not a worm in sight! It took two years of digging and adding compost to bring the worms back.

Worms are one of your best co-workers, as they turn over and mix the soil and break down organic lumps. Encourage them!

Buying in

If you are growing in containers or filling beds or raised beds from scratch, you may need to buy in your soil/compost initially. In time, you will be able to use your home-made compost, but this will take at least six months from your start-off point to be ready to use.

So what to buy and where to buy from? It goes without saying that the soil should be organic. There are a number of suppliers of organic compost on the Internet, and prices can vary considerably. It is common sense to use soil from your own area or as near as possible, so this may reduce your range further.

One fairly recent source is the more enlightened local councils. My own city (Plymouth) has set up an excellent recycling scheme using all the green waste collected from the homes in the area and the leaves and grass cuttings from council activities (e.g. parks, verges). If your town doesn't do this, work on them. It is good organic practice.

Wherever you buy it from, be sure that it is soil-based compost, not peat-based. Peat is becoming increasingly rare and should therefore be used sparingly. It is still needed for ericaceous compost, which is a more acidic mix for growing azaleas, rhododendrons, etc. It is not essential for general growing, and, in containers, the watering may turn it even more acidic, and your compost will end up mostly peat again.

So, choose a general, soil-based, organic compost from a reputable source (if you know them personally, even better). Be very cautious if it is described as having "soil enrichers" added, unless you know exactly what they are. If it's good quality, it doesn't need anything added to it.

If you already have some soil but it's not very good or very much, mix it in with the bought compost. Never waste anything you can get for free! If you can also add some farmyard manure, this will help too (and the farmer or stables will usually be pleased for you to take it). A good rule of thumb for the mixture: one part farmyard manure, one part poor garden soil (two parts if it's good) and three parts quality compost. Mix well together and fill your planters.

Why a compost heap?

Almost all the recent reports about the increase in diseases and pests in fruit and vegetables agree on one thing – when home-made, organic compost is used exclusively, the soil is totally healthy and productive, as are the crops, and nothing harmful is released into the atmosphere. So, it makes health sense, as well as economic sense, to make your own compost.

But doesn't it take up a lot of space? Well, the answer has to be "Yes – and no!"

If you have a lot of space and want to make lots of compost, then do so. But it can still be produced if space is limited. For smaller areas, there are compact, plastic compost bins on the market which fit into an area about one meter square. They are quite self-contained and lidded, so there should be no smell even if sited near the house. They will last for many years, can produce usable compost in about four to six months and can be sited in shady areas, where it is difficult to grow anyway.

If you have more room, square compost bins made of wood are probably the most convenient method. Build at least two so that one can be composting whilst the other is being filled. Make them as big as you have room for.

You can start composting at any time of year, but the real work will be done within the heap, from spring onwards, as the air gets warmer. If you have room to build a really big heap (I mean *really, really* big say 20'/6 m across!!)), then the composting process will produce its own heat, even in the middle of winter, and so perpetuate itself.

You've got your bin or heap set up ready; now what do you put into it to make compost?

Simply anything which was once growing and which will rot if left long enough. To get you started, here are a few ideas:

From the garden

- **Mown grass – be sure to scatter and mix them with other things, rather than put in a thick layer**
- **Prunings from shrubs – cut them into small bits or shred them if they are very woody**
- **Dead heads, dead plants and dead leaves**

- Old vegetable plants after the crop has been picked
- Weeds (but see allotment tip below)
- Ashes from bonfires
- Old soil or compost from pots and containers

From the house

- Fruit and vegetable peelings and skins
- Outer discarded leaves of vegetables (e.g. cabbage, lettuce, carrot tops) and stalks
- Pulp left after juicing
- Tea leaves, tea bags, coffee grounds
- Newspapers, telephone directories (without the glossy covers) – they are best shredded, but at least tear them up roughly
- Paper bags, wrappings, envelopes (not with windows), letters, cardboard packaging and cartons, egg boxes/trays
- Egg shells, cheese rinds
- Old cooked vegetables, including rice and pasta (there is some doubt about meat and fish because it attracts a variety of vermin and animals, but you may be safe with a lidded bin)
- Coal or wood ashes from fires or charcoal ash from barbecues

From the office

- **Shredded paper (not glossy)**
- **Pencil shavings**

Give it a go. It's a superb way of reducing rubbish which would otherwise go to landfill sites and puts all the goodness where it needs to be – back in the soil.

> Allotment tip:
> if you have dug up big weeds (e.g. dandelion, dock) you must ensure they are dead or they will regrow in the compost. Lay them on a flagstone or path, in full sun until they look "cooked" (about 1–2 days), and then put into the compost.

Do I have to dig?

Once again, the answer is "Yes – and no!" or possibly even "maybe". It does depend on what you are starting with.

a) Yes, you do.

If you are starting with land that has pernicious weeds in it (e.g. bramble, convolvulus, ground elder, dandelion, dock, nettle), you must get rid of them before you begin anything else. They must be removed completely – follow the roots till they are all out. Even the smallest piece of root left in the ground will grow a new plant and you'll never be free of them

As most spraying is not an option when growing organically, digging them out is the only answer. It is a good job for a crisp, dry winter's day and will get you really warmed up. Use a fork and don't try to do it all at once, particularly if you are not used to physical work. Set yourself an area to clear and do it. If you can organise friends and family to help, so much the better.

Having dug up the weeds, it is often best to burn them. You can't put them in the compost heap as they are, and there may be too many to "cook" (as above). The ashes can be dug into the ground or put into the compost.

If you have heavy clay, or compacted or disused soil, digging it over to let air in is a useful practice. It is best done in late autumn/fall or early winter and then left rough. If you have a lot of land, a hired rotivator makes the job easier.

To be really keen, you can "double dig" – a system of turning over and moving a spade's-depth quantity of soil and adding goodness at the same time. Dig a trench across the plot, about as deep as the size of your spade blade. Put the soil lifted on top of the earth (or into a barrow if you are in the edge). If you want, put a layer of compost or manure into the trench. Go backwards one step and dig again, this time putting the lifted soil into the previous trench. Carry on backwards to the end of the plot and then put the soil in the barrow or heap into the last trench.

This is a really good way to prepare new ground (and it only needs doing once).

b) No, you don't.

The recent school of thought says that it is better not to dig and disturb the soil too much. The mulch/no till system (as practised by the Strawbridge family in *It Isn't Easy Being Green*) works very well on fallow land, old lawn areas or ex–garden beds with no pernicious weeds.

To utilise this method, cut down any tall growth with a scythe, strimmer or similar (in my old garden, the boys had a great time with machetes). Then mow hard with any kind of lawn mower. If you don't have a mower, then hand cut as close to the ground as possible. Cover the whole area with a thick layer of cardboard and newspaper and soak it well, to help it rot down. Then cover that with a thick layer of compost or good topsoil. You can plant straight into these beds as appropriate for your seeds or plants.

If you are in no rush, you can cover a patch with old carpet and leave it for six- to twelve months. The weight of the carpet will exclude light and effectively stop weeds growing. Remove the carpet, and the ground is ready to use (a method introduced by Bob Flowerdew many years ago, and very radical at the time, but embraced now).

As your growing area matures and you keep on adding organic matter to it, the worm population will increase. In time, they will "dig" your garden for you.

Seeds – the very beginning

The seed is the beginning of life for a plant, and it is logical to begin organic growing with organic seed. There are suppliers of organic seeds on the Internet, and most tend to supply their own country or locale. This is logical, as the seeds will be more successful growing under similar conditions.

Organic seed tends to be a bit more expensive than non-organic (it has taken longer to produce and is subject to more tests and checks). That said, a packet of vegetable seed is a really good value. One packet of carrot seed costing about £1.75/$3.50, will provide more than enough carrots to feed a family of four through the summer. Compare that to buying carrots every week!

In fact, some seeds will be more than you need. If you are not planning to grow large quantities (or have limited space), a full packet of pea seeds will be more than you need. Most seeds, if stored properly, will save for another year, but their fertility will be reduced.

Growers usually prefer to use fresh seed each year, to be sure. So, rather than waste half a packet of seeds, why not share with a friend, and you can both reduce your growing costs?

To reduce costs even further, save seed from your own crops for the following year. Either allow one or two plants to produce flowers (say cabbage or onion), or leave a few pea or bean pods unpicked. When they are brown but still closed, collect and store in a paper bag in a dry place (not plastic, as it "sweats," and the moisture causes the seeds to rot).

You may find that the very tiny seeds, such as carrot, radish, lettuce, etc., are rather fiddly and difficult to collect. It may be easier to leave these to the professionals and simply enjoy the produce.

Fruit trees and plants

Planting a fruit tree or bush is making a commitment for a number of years. An apple, plum or pear tree, planted in open ground, will provide fruit (and shade, leaves for compost and pleasure for you) for twenty- to thirty years with minimal attention.

These trees need some space, so will suit a medium-sized garden. If space is limited or you are growing in containers, you will need to buy specialist, dwarf varieties.

When buying fruit trees, you will find that they are categorised by a a number and description, based on how vigorously the rootstock (see chapter 3) grows in open land. Here's a quick reference:

- M27 grows to a maximum of 1.8 m/6' (smaller in containers). A very "dwarf" variety.
- M9 grows to a maximum of 3 m/10'. A "dwarf" variety.
- M26 grows to a maximum of 3.6 m/11.5'. A "semi-dwarf" variety.

Any other numbers produce full-sized trees. There are also some "patio" trees on the market, specially produced for growing in containers.
Even smaller trees, grown in containers, should have a fruitful life of about eight- to ten years. An additional advantage is that they can move house with you.

Whatever you choose to grow, there are just two basic principles.

1. **Buy from a registered organic, reputable source.**
2. **Buy the best you can afford. The quality will pay off.**

Do not be tempted by special offers in supermarkets, DIY centres, general stores, etc. Although they may be cheaper, they will almost certainly not be grown organically. Worse, you may import pests or diseases in the compost, which will certainly affect the tree and possibly other crops as well.

If you are buying directly from the grower or an accredited outlet, do not be afraid to check exactly what you are buying. Gently lift the tree/bush out of its pot and look at the roots. They should be numerous and nearly filling the pot; a mixture of a few dark, strong anchor roots and a lot of paler "feeder" roots; although filling the pot, they should not be running round and round the pot (pot bound).

If buying by mail order, send back anything which has inadequate roots or looks sickly – a reputable grower will understand.

When you get your tree/shrub, put it into a bucket of water, pot and all, for an hour or two. Then plant it out into its hole or container. Add a small spadeful of manure or compost directly under the roots. If it has been grown in a pot, gently loosen the roots to encourage them to grow outwards.

Any book or programme with Alan Titchmarsh will show you sound basics for planting trees, as well as their subsequent care. He also follows a piece of folklore which I was taught as a child (must be the Yorkshire influence!). When you have planted your tree, filled in the hole or pot and pressed the soil down firmly, take hold of the trunk with both hands, give it a gentle shake and say, "Grow, tree, grow," in a firm voice. Then give it (and yourself) a good drink – water for the tree, whatever you fancy for yourself!

Water! Water!

Previously we have looked at the plants' need for water. Now let's look at where it comes from.

This may seem a naïve question, "Where does it come from?", but I bet you gave one of two answers: a) from the tap/faucet, or b) from the sky. Both, of course, are correct. So what? Might I suggest that, from a food point of view, b) is the better option.

We tend to take fresh drinking water in our homes for granted. Many gardeners fill their watering cans or use hosepipes from this domestic supply, without much thought. But domestic water costs money AND it has already been processed for consumption. It is common sense to use it for human consumption.

Plants don't care about water being processed – they can do it for themselves. They don't care if it contains dust, dead insects, soil, bird droppings, etc – they can deal with it. So why waste expensive, treated water on plants?

What plants do have problems with are the added chemicals which have been used to purify the water for people. On average, domestic water contains at least chlorine and fluoride and possibly traces of many others. The proportions are safe to drink, but they will change in a plant, and may well accumulate over a long period.

It is much better to use rainwater for your plants. But first, you have to collect it.

If you have some space and a "fall pipe" from the guttering around the roof, there are gadgets available from DIY stores to divert rainwater from the fall pipe into a container. They are cheap, easy to fit, and very efficient. My own water barrel fills in about two hours of rain. All the rain which hits my roof goes into it (when the barrel is full, the gadget lets the water back down the pipe).

If you don't have access to a pipe from the roof, put a bucket, bowl or similar container where it can catch the rain. Even if space is really limited, such as on a balcony, you can rig up a system of very large funnel tied to the to the outside of the balcony, attached to a length of hosepipe which runs into a container (bucket, watering can, 4 litre recycled bottle, etc.).

One rarely considered source is recycled "grey" water. This is water which has been used previously for washing dishes or in baths or showers. A bowl of washing-up water can be used on plants. They don't mind the soap, but to be absolutely safe, use a biodegradable washing liquid or shower gel.

Whatever you use, it makes economic and environmental sense to save water wherever you can.

Nuisances

Animals

However much we love them, family pets can be a nuisance to the gardener. My own dog loves lying in the sun on top of a cushion of plants – not too bad when it is daisies, but a blessed nuisance when it is lettuces.

Many pets will dig in soil (even in pots) for a variety of reasons, and this will loosen the plants' roots and prevent them growing properly, or at all. So, you have to find ways of protecting your growing area. At its simplest, a fence or wall round will protect from most activities, although a really persistent offender will still get round it.

Remember, pet rabbits are still rabbits! They will eat anything green.

Animal droppings are another potential problem. Both cat and dog urine can be very acidic and damaging to plants. Another reason to separate animals and crops.

Poo is a universal problem. Although we use and recommend farm manure, this is from herbivores (leaf-eaters). Cats and dogs are carnivores.

(meat eaters). Most people are reluctant to include pet droppings into their compost heap, although there is no real evidence that it is necessarily bad.

Personally, I have buried my dogs' poo in the flowerbeds for many years, with no apparent ill-effects. I have to admit, though, that I do not put it into the compost or bury it in the vegetable beds (but the dogs aren't allowed in the vegetable garden anyway).

This is one occasion when the choice is yours.

Family
A minor nuisance which you may not be aware of is your own family. Without any malice aforethought, kids (and adults) can cause damage. A well-aimed football can smash the stems of beans or brussels sprouts, and they will not re-grow; heavy feet can flatten young crops. Your best bet is training. In fact, if you involve the children in the growing process, they will be careful naturally.

Hygiene is not just for the house

Garden hygiene is as important as any other kind, particularly if you are using recycled items (and I hope you are). As a grower, it is the benefit of good hygiene to the plants, rather than to humans, which concerns us here.

All plants have their own specific diseases, micro-organisms and peculiarities. The majority of all of these have no affect whatever on the plant itself or the consumer later. A healthy plant will cope with and offset most of the problems which hit it.

Problems arise when one type of plant is introduced to a disease from another type or a more virulent form of its own type, both of which it doesn't have any defence against. The most common way this happens is through plants bought in their pots. This is why we recommend growing from seed rather than buying half-grown plants.

Diseases can linger in used pots, even from plants we have raised ourselves. The simple routine is to ensure all pots, trays or containers are thoroughly cleaned. It is a simple task of washing everything in hot soapy water – use a biodegradable detergent to save rinsing. It's a great job for the children on a warm day.

A plant's individual diseases can be left in the soil after the plant has been lifted. If the same type is planted in the same soil, the amount left increases. Done over a number of years, the result is such a concentration of the disease that the plants can no linger fight it naturally.

Any monoculture (constantly growing a single crop on the same soil) will ultimately cause problems with the crop. The Irish potato famine is probably the best-known example. Potato blight built up in the soil till it infected everything which was planted in it. Even today, similar problems are becoming evident in monocultures. At present it is a lessening of cropping, and many growers are offsetting this with additional chemical treatment. It is a cause for concern, as such practices cannot be continued indefinitely without serious damage to the soil and environment.

This why we always recommend that you rotate your crops and grow them in different places each year. If your growing space is in containers, empty them, wash (as above) and refill with new soil or compost.

Protection rackets

If you live in a cooler climate, there will be some crops you will not be able to grow, unless you can provide protection (the most obvious are peppers and chillies, peaches, grapes and citrus fruits). The most common form of protection is the greenhouse. Most gardens, however small, can probably take a greenhouse, somewhere.

But what if you are working with a small paved area or balcony? There are plastic covered mini-greenhouses, which are about 1 meter square x 1.5 meters tall. They have shelves which will hold seed trays, seedlings, and small pots. (Drop a hint for your next birthday present!)

Traditionally, gardeners have used "cold frames" for protection. These usually stand at ground level and consist of low walls with liftable glass tops. They are unheated and used for the protection of young plants till planting-out time. My neighbour has built one in his yard out of concrete blocks (two high) against his house wall, and the "lid" is made from two old windows. It works a treat.

To go even smaller, plants can be protected by a cloche – a domed, clear cover over a single plant. Here your recycling comes in : a 2 litre drink bottle with the bottom cut off will cover a plant until it is quite large; a 4 litre bottle (water/milk) will cover a whole patch of seedlings or a whole plant.
Putting plants under glass will extend your growing season considerably. By starting seeds early, under cover, you will be able to plant out half-grown vegetables in the spring – so, earlier crops!

Where you are planting seed directly into the ground, you can bring that forward by warming up the soil with a tunnel cloche. This is clear plastic sheet over metal/plastic hoops stuck into the ground. It gives protection to the soil against frosts and stops it getting waterlogged.

Cloche kits can be bought and are not very expensive. It is even cheaper to build your own from wire coat hangers, bent into a curve and covered with cheap polythene sheeting.

So, when do I start?

Most growing starts in the spring. (But also see chapter 10). Your seed packets will give you sowing times for both in the open and under cover. There is little point starting before the ground has started to warm up – the seeds won't germinate and you'll get frustrated.

> Allotment tip:
> To work out if the soil is warming up, check out the hedges and deciduous shrubs in your area. When you see buds appearing and the bushes have a greenish tinge, rather than brown, it's time!

But there is preparation to be done before sowing. You may have to prepare the ground, build beds or paths, dig over or add soil or compost. All these can be done, weather permitting, at any time.

So what if you are a bit late starting – let's say, early summer? Well, there are still crops which can be started then: late potatoes, salad (plant every two weeks till the end of August) and, most importantly, begin the winter vegetables (cabbage, leeks, broccoli).

If it's even later – nearly autumn – this is time to think of planting fruit trees and shrubs. It is too late to really start growing, but you can plan for next spring and, maybe, start some onion, broad beans or garlic seeds. Really, there is something to do whenever you begin, even if it's getting catalogues and ordering seeds.

The main thing is to START NOW. Do what you can as soon as you can, and start reaping the benefits. So, let's get to some specific growing tips and ideas to get you underway.

DOWN TO EARTH

CHAPTER SIX

A Child Could Do It:
Herbs and Salad

CHAPTER SIX

A good introduction to food growing, particularly in limited space, is salad. Almost all salad crops are easy to grow, need little fuss and take up relatively little space. They are excellent crops for children to undertake, as most grow quite quickly and it is very exciting to see the seeds producing plants "before your very eyes".

For the purposes of this chapter, we will define "salad" as the sort of summer crops which we generally eat uncooked – lettuce, cucumber, radishes, spring onions, with a diversion into peppers for those of you with a greenhouse and a bit of adventure. (Yes, you can add other items such as carrots and celery to your salad, but these will be covered in other chapters.)

Generally, salad crops need fairly rich soil or good growing compost (if in containers), warmth (though not necessarily direct sunlight) and plenty of water. They will grow well in containers and, if planted in succession, will last throughout the summer. They rarely store (though tomatoes can be processed and saved), so are eaten and enjoyed in their season. It is possible to extend your season by growing winter salad in a greenhouse, but we will assume for now that we are talking about summer crops.

Containers

Did you ever grow mustard and cress on a piece of blotting paper when you were little? If you did, can you remember the pleasure of seeing those little shoots appearing and growing at quite a rate? If not, you don't know what you've missed. So, how about remedying this situation and introducing your children to this pleasure, at the same time?

Simply place a double piece of blotting paper or a piece of cotton cloth (a J cloth will work at a pinch) in a shallow tray, such as the sort of tray you get meat in at the supermarket. Damp it well, and sow the mustard and cress seed thinly all over it. Keep it damp – it is important not to let it dry out – and watch the magic.

But for those of you who are beyond this basic stage, containers provide an ideal situation for growing salad. Lettuce, radish and spring onions do well in troughs. They do not need very deep soil. You can use wooden fruit boxes, lined with plastic, in the same way. Make sure that there are plenty of holes in the lining, to avoid the soil getting waterlogged (salad needs water, but it cannot swim!).

A large pot or ornamental container can take quite a variety of crops – you can plant a complete salad in a large pot. Place a "bush" tomato plant in the centre, and surround it with a few lettuces, radishes, onions and (if it is a big pot) a bit of parsley. It will look stunning and feed you, all at the same time.

For those with a little more space, a "Grobag" will grow three tomato plants. They will need some support as they grow. Traditionally, growers have placed a tall cane (5'/1.5 m) behind each tomato plant, and tied the plant to it as it rows. The "Grobag" may not provide enough depth of soil to support a cane, so a good system is to place the bag at the foot of a wall and provide wires or strings on the wall to act as supports.

Recycled plastic bags folded back to half way and filled with compost (see chapter 6) will take two tomato plants and supports (and probably a bit of parsley or a few radishes as well). This is also a much cheaper option.
Whatever you choose, do not be afraid to plant your salad components fairly close to each other – they are very sociable.

Timing

One of the minor hassles with salad growing is that no two crops grow at the same rate. It is very difficult to get everything ready to eat together. Radishes are rapid growers – great for the children! They will be up and ready to eat in a couple of weeks. But the lettuce and spring onions will take twice as long, and the tomatoes and cucumber, considerably longer.

You may have to accept that you will be buying tomatoes initially whilst eating the rest of the salad which you have grown. (It is usually the tomatoes which are the nuisance, as you can't hurry them.)

For the rest, successional sowing (see chapter 3) is essential. It is so easy to sow half a packet of lettuce seed and then find you have thirty lettuces ready to eat at the same time. This may make you very popular with your friends and neighbours, who will be getting gifts of lettuce, but is a bit of a waste of seed. So, only plant a few at any one time, and leave about two weeks between each planting.

Start your lettuce first, and the radish and onions about four weeks afterwards. In theory they should be ready just about together (although years of experience have taught me that "sod's law" is very common in growing – so do the best you can and enjoy what you get when you get it!)

Salad does not transplant well, so you will need to sow where it will grow. This does mean that you cannot sow seed until the ground is warm enough. Too early and the seed will not germinate and may well rot – a waste of your time, energy and seed. The exception is tomatoes and cucumbers, which can be started in a greenhouse or on a window ledge, and grown until they are about 6"/15 cm tall. They can then be hardened off (see chapter 3) if you are growing them outside, or potted up for the greenhouse.

Under cover work

A greenhouse, plastic mini-greenhouse, cold frame or warm window ledge really comes into its own when you are starting off your salad crops. All salad seeds are very sensitive to temperature, particularly lettuce. They will not germinate in the first place until it is warm enough; if they begin to grow and the temperature falls, they will give up; if it is too hot, they go dormant, so will not germinate at all.

So, consistency of temperature and reasonable warmth are a must. A greenhouse or other protection will provide this for you.

But not everyone has space, even for a mini-greenhouse, and has no option but to plant directly into the ground or container. If this is your case, watch the outside temperature, and do not be tempted to plant too early. If you in any doubt, give your seeds some protection by covering with growers' fleece or cloches. Containers can be covered with a sheet of glass or plastic sheeting until the seedlings can look after themselves (this also helps to conserve moisture).

A greenhouse or frame can help to extend your growing season considerably. Planting "cut and come again" varieties of lettuce will give you salad through the winter. (These are types which do not produce a solid heart, but just lots of fairly loose leaves. You can cut as much as you need and leave the rest to carry on growing.)

Alternatively, sow lettuce in the autumn for picking early the following spring. They will grow very slowly and be ready early, but this method does not suit all varieties. Good types for overwintering are "Valdor" and "Little Gem", but you can try all sorts to see what works for you – just sow a few seeds of each.

Tomatoes

Everyone knows what a tomato looks like – don't they? Have you checked out the supermarket shelves at the height of the salad season?

Tomatoes are red. Or orange. Or yellow. Or even purple!

Tomatoes are round. Or plum shaped. Or oval. They are the size of cherries, or plums, or tennis balls; are smooth or knobbly skinned; are sweet or bland.

In other words, there is a massive variety in this most versatile vegetable (fruit?). A wander through the pages of a seed catalogue is a journey of exploration. There seem to be more new types every year. So where do you begin?

First, decide on the space you are prepared to allocate to growing tomatoes. Is it in a greenhouse or outdoors? Are you growing in containers or the open ground? How big a space have you? That decided, you can pick a variety which fits your conditions.

> Tip:
> When you decide, remember to check the size of the plant as well as the size of the tomatoes it produces. There are some cherry tomato plants which will grow to 5'/1.5 m tall. Some "bush" types can take up a spread of 3'/1 m.

Technically, there are two types of tomato plant – vine and bush. On vine types, the fruits grow from the main stem along a short side stem, called a truss. The plants will grow quite tall – up to 5'/1.5 m – and will need to be supported by a tall enough stick, cane, wire or string. Side shoots are removed and the plant is "stopped" (see chapter 3) when enough flower stems (trusses) have formed – usually about five. They grow quite happily in containers or "Grobags "(though these will need a bit more attention), and are best grown in a greenhouse.

Bush varieties are much more compact, with a number of side branches, with the flowers at the end of the stems. Once the flowers appear, this stops the stem growing, so more side stems are produced. The effect is of a small flowering shrub. They will grow outdoors in either containers or open ground. Generally, they crop earlier than the vine types and can produce a large amount of tomatoes.

Whichever type you choose, you can start off the seeds indoors, in a greenhouse or on a window ledge. Do not be tempted to sow very early – it is no good having young plants ready to transplant into the open if the weather is not warm enough for them to grow. Generally sow in mid-spring, but you can be a bit earlier (say mid-March) in milder areas. The most convenient method is to put two seeds in a small pot in a warmish place. As they grow, pull out the weaker of the two and leave the strong one to carry on. By the time the seedlings are about 1"/2½ cm high, transfer the pots to a light place if they are not there already.

As the seedlings grow, still in their mild germination area, transplant them into bigger pots (say, 2½"/6 cm). When the plants' roots have filled the pot, they are ready for planting out. If you are growing vine tomatoes in a greenhouse, then you simply transplant them into their growing area, large pot or "Grobag". If you are growing bush tomatoes outdoors, you will need to harden them off (see chapter 3) for about two weeks before putting them in their final growing place.

As they grow, the watering of tomatoes, wherever you grow them, becomes critical. They are thirsty plants and need watering every day. It is no good soaking them one day and then neglecting them for the next two – every day!! One result of erratic watering is that the growing fruits split, as if they have been cut with a knife. This happens because the skins cannot cope with the sudden up-rush of water after they have been dry. This is very common in outdoor varieties, if the grower has relied on the weather only to provide.

Other than water, all they will now need is warmth. Note: warmth, not necessarily direct sunlight. Where possible, place your tomatoes in a sheltered area. If you are not sure, you can always build a small windbreak round the plant(s) using sticks and clear plastic or growers' fleece.

In the greenhouse, if you are growing vine tomatoes, you will need to remove the side shoots. These appear in the fork between the main stem and a leaf, and will look like baby plants with two leaves (which is what they are). Simply nip them off once they are big enough to get a good grip on them. You won't confuse them with the trusses; they appear out of the main stem on a space between the leaves.

Some growers also remove the lower leaves once the fruit is showing. It is believed to allow more nutrients to the crop. I have done both methods – removing and leaving – and have not noticed much difference to the crop. But the plants do take up less room without the bigger, lower leaves.

Problems

If you are growing from seed, you should experience very few problems with your plants. Very few pests show any interest in them.

Outdoors, you are at the mercy of the weather, so your tomatoes may be slower to ripen if the weather is cooler.

The only real problem is *blight* – which you could import if you buy young plants from another source. It is the same fungal disease which affects potatoes (they are the same botanical family as tomatoes). You will know if your plants have blight – brown spots will appear on the leaves and then spread until the whole leaf is covered and dying. Then the fruits will be affected the same way. There may be grey, fluffy fungus growth on the leaves as well.

There is little you can do about blight, other than spray with Bordeaux mixture (see appendix 1) in advance and throughout warm, damp weather. The best prevention is to reduce the risk by ensuring the plants do not get too wet and humid (ideal conditions for the disease to flourish). If you see any signs, remove the leaves immediately and burn them (do NOT add them to the compost heap). Also make sure that there is no debris or mess in the area which spores can cling to – general garden hygiene.

Before you get too panicky, I must say that I have never experienced blight on either tomatoes or potatoes in all the years I have grown vegetables, either indoors or out. So be alert, but do not get paranoid – and grow from seed!

If you are growing in containers, "Grobags" or have supplemented your greenhouse soil with bought compost, you may experience a slowing-down of growth or ripening when the tomatoes are nearly fully grown. This is usually accompanied by lighter patches appearing on the leaves and a general look of ill-health.

Most commercial, general-purpose compost is based on peat, which is acidic. As you water the plants, the nutrients are taken up or washed away and the peat is left behind. This means that the compost is getting steadily more acidic with time. This is not good news for the tomatoes.

The remedy is both simple and old-fashioned – Epsom salts! Epsom salts is an alkaline – magnesium sulphate – used on people to bathe swellings. Simply add a dessertspoonful to a watering can and water in the usual way. It offsets the acidity, and the plants will perk up in a few days.

To prevent this situation, use peat-free compost or your own home-made stuff.

Harvesting

Pick your crop when they are nice and red all over (or yellow or purple). Look for colour rather than size. They are best eaten soon after picking. For a taste explosion, eat immediately; your taste buds will thank you! They will store in the fridge for about the same time as bought ones.

Towards the end of the season, when the weather starts to get cooler, your tomatoes may not ripen. In this case, pick the fruit even though it is green, and put them to ripen in a warm place. A window ledge which doesn't get too much direct sunlight, but is warm, is good, as is the airing cupboard.

If even that does not work, then make green tomato chutney, which you can enjoy through the winter.

If you have more fruit than you can cope with and cannot give any more away, either make a basic tomato sauce with onions, garlic (optional), a little basil and a little sugar. Cook all together until soft, liquidise and store in jars or bottles. It will also freeze very well. Alternatively, simply skin, liquidise and freeze as tomato juice for your breakfast.

Lettuce

A lettuce is basically a collection of leaves made mostly of water. They need warmth and sunlight, reasonably fertile soil and lots of water. They will grow almost anywhere in the summer months, and in many areas, with some protection, in the winter, provided they have water.

Do you detect a slight repetition here? Guess what is most important when growing lettuce? Correct – water!

Don't get paranoid – moisture retention will serve your purpose just as well as pouring water directly onto the plants. So long as they do not get too dry, you will be fine.

So, lettuces, they come in two types: those which form a dense "heart" of close-growing leaves, and those which are an open collection of leaves and much looser in shape.

The former are much liked by commercial growers as they last well and the customer gets quite a lot of lettuce for their money. However, they do need a great deal of water to produce, particularly the very dense types such as the iceberg or cos varieties. And they need a lot more care and attention.

The non-hearting varieties, and particularly the mini-lettuce, are, on the other hand, ideal for the domestic grower and smaller areas. Many can be used as "cut and come again" – taking just what you need and leaving the rest of the plant to carry on growing till the next meal. They do not take up too much room, and the moisture content can be maintained very easily with mulching and good soil

Whichever type you choose, it has to be accepted that lettuce is, largely, a summer crop (in the UK, at least). You can grow them in a greenhouse in the winter, but only if the temperature doesn't get too low – then you will have to heat the greenhouse, which increases your costs considerably.

> **If you are seriously thinking of heating a greenhouse to grow all year round, check out Richard Smallbridge's book, *It Isn't Easy Being Green*. He has a workable greenhouse heating system using a solar panel, a glass-filled heat sump and a small air pump. It is virtually free to use, after the initial capital outlay, and is very eco-friendly.**

The other snag is that lettuce seeds tend to germinate, grow and mature all at the same time. So, unless you are planning to give away lots of lettuce to your friends and neighbours, or breed rabbits, only plant a few at a time, about every two weeks. As the seed is very small, it might help to mix it with some dry sand; this should give you a finer spread of seed.

Generally, it is better to sow your seed directly where you are going to grow your lettuce. They do not take kindly to disturbance once they have started growing. If you have sown the seed too close (and it's very difficult not too), simply thin out the clumps as they grow. From about 3"/8 cm tall, they are perfectly edible, so need not be wasted.

If you do want to sow the seed early, use modules rather than seed trays, as you can then lift the whole seedling without too much disturbance. Plant the seedlings out before they have six leaves and plant with the leaves just above soil level. The depth is important: if the leaves are touching the soil, they may rot; too high, and they will not form a proper-shaped head.

In dry weather, or if the watering has been erratic, lettuce is inclined to "bolt" (see chapter 3). This is very obvious –instead of a round, low-growing collection of leaves, you will find that you have a fairly tall, straight stem growing skyward very quickly. Unfortunately, there is little you can do about this, so just add that plant to the compost heap and ensure all the others are watered regularly.

Many creatures also like lettuce, particularly slugs and snails. Use your normal methods of control, or cover with fleece, making sure it is well fastened to the ground (or they will get underneath).

If your growing area joins open country, you may have a rabbit problem. But you will already know about this, as wild rabbits will have attacked almost everything you plant. Fencing is the usual answer, but do be sure it is well buried into the ground – rabbits can dig and will go down up to 12"/30 cm to get under a barrier.

But, generally, lettuces are easy and relatively problem free. They are a fairly quickly growing crop, so the children will love them. Not long to wait before seeing results!

Radish

The radish is a brilliant crop to grow and an ideal plant for involving the children in the process. They grow very quickly and are easy to grow and pick, and most people enjoy eating them.

Radish seed is sown directly into the growing area (like lettuce, they do not transplant well). They will grow in most soils, although a fairly rich, well-manured soil will give better results and hold moisture. Sow just a few seeds, very thinly, every two weeks, water in and wait for the crop. The only ongoing care they will need is watering, if the weather is dry, and weeding.

As said above, radish grows very quickly – about two weeks from sowing to harvesting. So, you could well have a good crop of radish before anything else in the salad plot is ready. Successional sowings will allow the rest of the salad to catch up, and you can eat the radish on their own, anyway.

Because they grow so quickly, it is easy to end up with too many and the last ones get too big. This is one crop where big is not beautiful! A large radish is very fibrous and tastes woody; it is not a desirable food. So pick them when they are about 1.5"/4 cm long – you will know they are big enough when the top of the radish comes just out of the ground below the leaves. Hold the leaves, pull gently and try to get them to the table (it is very tempting to eat them there and then!).

There are some late summer/early winter varieties, particularly the Japanese varieties, which can give the more adventurous grower some fun. They tend to grow bigger and are much more like a turnip than a radish (though still with the slightly peppery taste). But they are grown on much the same way.

Radishes have few problems. Slugs and snails will nibble, as with any crop, and if you get cabbage root fly in the garden (see chapter 10), this can spread to the radishes. But, generally they are trouble-free. They will grow happily in containers; a small sprinkling of seed in a 6"/15 cm pot every two weeks will suit most growers. If you have a large family or are radish fanatics, make it a 10"/25 cm pot.

Most people start with the "French breakfast" type, which are long, or "Scarlet Globe", which are round. Both are very reliable and easy to grow. So get the youngsters going!

Peppers

Sweet peppers and chilli peppers (*Capsicum*) are warm climate plants, originating from round the Mediterranean and the Middle East. They need warmth to grow and ripen, and so, in the UK at any rate, tend to be grown in the greenhouse. It is possible to grow them outdoors, if you have a warm, protected place for them.

All types need fairly rich soil and a reasonable amount of water. But they do not like to be waterlogged, so good drainage is essential. Provide these conditions and they will grow in pots, "Grobags" or open soil. All will need some support – a cane for each plant (like tomatoes) is necessary, as the plants get quite top-heavy as the fruits develop. Water as you would tomatoes – every day, if indoors, rather than a lot of water sometimes, with gaps of nothing between.

Wherever you ultimately grow them, start the seed off indoors. They need some warmth to germinate and begin the growing process, so do not be tempted to start them too early – you will get no results. Once the seedlings can be handled, prick out into small pots (2″/5 cm), one seedling to each pot. Continue to grow them indoors until they are about 3″/8 cm tall, then either pot up into a bigger pot (4″/10 cm) or harden off to ready for planting outside. Plant the outdoor plants into their growing containers or space only after hardening off or the shock will be too much for them to cope with.

Other than support and water, peppers require very little attention as they grow. You can give them an occasional feeding with tomato food, but this is not essential and should not be done too often, as it will encourage the plant to produce leaves instead of fruits.

Peppers have few predators or diseases. Aphids may attack the growing tops and should be removed as soon as they are seen. In the greenhouse, you may get *Botrytis* (grey rot), a fungal disease, in damp and cold weather. It is recognisable by the pale grey fuzz covering the leaves or fruits.

Good general hygiene usually prevents this forming, but if your plants are infected, remove the infected parts immediately and destroy them (not for the compost heap). If the stem of the plant is affected, cut it back to good, healthy wood. The plant will do the rest.

Generally, in the UK and cooler countries, peppers do not grow as big as the ones we see in the shops (which are grown in hot countries). But they taste every bit as good. Pick them when they are ripe and have achieved an all-over red colour. If you have some semi-ripened fruits at the end of the season, you can probably finish them off on a window ledge, with the tomatoes.

Cucumber

Cucumbers belong to the *Cucurbit* family of plants, which also includes marrows, courgettes, melons and squashes.

Cucumbers, whether grown indoors or out, need slightly more attention than most salad crops. That said, they are well worth the effort for the considerably better flavour than anything you can buy.

Cucumbers are trailing (or climbing) plants, by nature. They are best grown up a support, which can be a wigwam of canes or a trellis, or fastened to wires. Then they will take up far less space, too.

Most cucumbers are grown in greenhouses or cold frames. These are smooth skinned, fairly long and do not need pollinating. Outdoor types are rough skinned (often with ridges along their length), shorter and stubbier, and DO need pollinating – if not pollinated by insects, you will have to do the honours (see later in this section). There is little to choose between indoor or outdoor types in terms of flavour.

All cucumber seed should be sown indoors. Plant two seeds to a small pot (2"/5 cm) and remove the weaker plantlet when they are about 3"/8 cm tall. (If you have lots of space or want lots of cucumbers, you can plant them all out). No cucumbers will tolerate frost, so do not be tempted to plant them out early; it is a waste of effort and plants. They will continue quite happily under glass until the time is right to be hardened off and then planted out.

If growing outdoors, make sure that the area you are planning to plant them in is well manured. They will even grow with their roots in the manure, so do not be stingy in preparing the ground. Once the young plants are in their growing place, mulch generously all round them with home-made compost or manure to give water retention and keep the ground warmer.

If space is not a problem, allow about 3 square feet/1 square metre for reach plant and let them spread as they will. If it is, then provide one cane/stick for each plant, and tie the growing plant against the support as it grows. When the stem reaches the top of the canes, pinch out the top to prevent further growth. The cucumbers will hang down the plant and ripen as they grow.

In the greenhouse, growing up canes or wires is the usual option, to use the space effectively. It is not advisable to grow cucumbers near other, similar plants, such as squash or melon, as they may get cross-pollinated by the others, which will spoil the cucumber fruits.

> **West Country growing tip:**
> **Do NOT grow cucumbers in a greenhouse which houses a grape vine. The cucumbers have a detrimental effect on the vine, and you will get no grapes! It doesn't bother the cucumbers.**

Harvest your cucumbers when the sides of the fruits are parallel and the fruits are a fresh green. If they begin to turn yellow, they are getting rather old. Do not be tempted to pick too early, as the fruits will be bitter to taste.

Cucumbers suffer from the usual problems: slugs, snails and aphid, but these can be largely avoided by good hygiene and cultivation practices. Watering steadily, as with most summer vegetables, is essential, but do not be tempted to overwater. Although they are largely composed of water, cucumbers do not actually like to be too wet. Proper watering will avoid the humid conditions which may cause fungus diseases.

Cold summer weather (especially if it is also damp) can cause premature rot in half-grown fruits. The fruit looks normal, but the end away from the stem becomes soft and mushy (it is not pleasant). Pick the fruits, throw them away (you can't salvage anything) and put it down to experience. The plant will not be affected and should produce further flowers and fruits, anyway. (This condition can also affect courgettes and young marrows.)

Good hygiene in the greenhouse should avoid problems with indoor varieties, which are relatively trouble free.

Pollination

If you are growing your cucumbers outdoors, the flowers will need to be pollinated to produce fruits. Generally, the insects will do this job for you, but some years there are fewer insects (usually because of damp or cool conditions), so you have the job. It is great fun!

Your plants will produce two sorts of flowers which look very similar to each other. They will be yellowish and about 2"/5 cm long with oval-shaped petals. But the female flower has an obvious attachment behind the flower. This is the potential fruit, and it is thick and about as long as the flower itself. The male flower simply has a stalk.

On a still day, pick an opened male flower and push it gently into an opened female flower. Gently move it around a little to transfer the pollen to the female, and then let nature take its course.

Greenhouse varieties are all-female and do not need this process. In fact, pollination will actually be detrimental to the fruits, even from the same plant. There should not be male flowers produced, but it happens sometimes in cooler weather, so if that is the case, simply remove the male flowers and throw them away.

Growing tip: Generally, if you plant the cucumbers close together, outdoors, you will get more male flowers than female; further apart gives the opposite result.

Herbs

Herbs were probably the first plants to be cultivated when man settled down to living and growing in one place. They are certainly one of the oldest recorded crops, and have a long and fascinating history in both food and medicine.

From our point of view, herbs have the added advantage of being really easy to grow.

Many herbs originated in the Middle East and are spread all round the Mediterranean. So, they are used to the hotter, drier climate of those areas. However, they adapt very readily to all different sorts of climates and conditions.

If you have been to any Mediterranean country on holiday, you will have noticed the wild plants growing by roads, in cracks in walls and at the edges of fields. Do you remember the smell? I bet you do. And did you say, "That reminds of something"? Well, it's a safe bet that it was some form of everyday herb, probably thyme, marjoram or sage. If they can grow wild in Spain, they can certainly grow in your garden or on your window ledge.

Traditional herb gardens are a regular feature of stately homes. In the older ones, they are known as "knot" gardens, because the beds were arranged in elaborate knot shapes, usually surrounded by low hedges. Herbs were an essential part of cookery and the basis of all domestic medicine until relatively recently.

Modern requirements are much less. Very few people make their own medicines, so the main use is in cookery. I have a friend whose perpetual comment is, "I don't like herbs. I don't eat any of them." It's odd, but he puts mint sauce on his lamb and parsley sauce on his fish and has sage and onion stuffing in the turkey. Doesn't eat herbs, eh?

But, generally, herbs are an acceptable part of modern cooking, and the increased popularity of Italian and Spanish cookery has encouraged this. But, that said, the average cook does not use large amounts of herbs, even in a Continental diet. So, they are ideal for growing in small quantities in easily accessible places, near the kitchen. Pots and containers are ideal, as are window boxes and troughs.

Within the garden/growing area, they will cohabit with practically everything, and some of the stronger scented ones are very beneficial to other crops (garlic next to carrots and parsley next to celery). They make good borders to beds or containers and can be used to fill odd spaces between other crops.

Not all herbs can overwinter in the UK, even in the milder areas. But some that can and will flourish are thyme, sage, marjoram, bay, rosemary and, of course, mint. Others can be outdoors in the summer, but need protection through the colder months. These include parsley, dill and tarragon, although they are probably easier to grow fresh each spring from seed.

So, decide which herbs you will use, and begin sowing the seeds in the spring in trays in the greenhouse or on your window ledge. As a starter pack, you can probably have fun with parsley, thyme, sage and dill.
The easiest of all these is parsley. Unusual for herbs, parsley prefers rich soil, although it is not fussy about sunlight and will grow in partial shade. It is sociable with almost anything else in the garden, and will flourish in containers, either alone or with other vegetables.

Parsley makes an ideal edging plant, as it doesn't get too tall, so place a few plantlets around the edge of your salad or runner bean pot. Alternatively, put it along the edge of the vegetable (or flower) beds.

Parsley will rarely overwinter – the leaves die back once the temperature starts to fall – but you can prolong its growing time by covering the plant with a cloche or similar protection.

Thyme, marjoram and sage all do well in UK gardens. In fact, in milder areas, they can grow to bush proportions if not kept in check. They will grow in all sorts of soils, but do not like very wet conditions. The ideal situation is a sunny, well-drained spot in fairly light soil. (I have thyme and sage plants in my own garden which are now four years old and still going strong.)

All three do very well in containers and indoors. They will not mind the heat of a kitchen and will flourish on a sunny window ledge. They will even make a decorative (and useful) plant in a conservatory, although they will probably need slightly more watering because of the greater heat.

Leaves will be available throughout the winter, although they may look rather bedraggled. This is quite normal. In the spring, when there are a few new shoots showing, simply cut off all the top of the plant. A straight cut with garden shears is the easiest. It looks brutal, but the plant will recover quite quickly, and more light and air can get to the new growth at the bottom of the plant.

As these plants get older, they will get more "shrubby" in appearance and nature. This will not affect the younger leaves too much, but the quality of the herb will diminish with age. It may be an idea to take cuttings from the tops of new growth to provide replacement plants.

> **Technical moment – cuttings:**
>
> Count down three sets of leaves from the top of the stem, and cut just underneath the third set. Then remove these bottom leaves carefully without damaging the stem itself. Place the "cuttings" around the outside of a small pot of compost, fairly close together, water gently and put on a warm window ledge or in the greenhouse.
>
> Keep the compost damp, but not sopping wet, until you notice the plants growing or small roots appearing out of the bottom of the pot. Then put each new plant in a small pot of its own, and grow on.
>
> Only put cuttings around the edge, not in the centre. I don't know why they don't grow in the centre, but they don't!

Bay trees are a fashionable pot plant, and are seen (usually neatly clipped into a ball) in hotels and restaurants and by front doors. In these cases, the leaves are rarely used in their herbal capacity, which is a waste!

Bay is a tough Mediterranean shrub, whose leaves add flavour to many dishes. It is used to fairly harsh conditions, hot sun and poor soil, so a plant pot is no hardship and the average garden is positively luxurious. It does well in the UK, though slightly better in the south than the north. In colder regions, it may have to be taken indoors for the winter, or wrapped up as protection. In my southern garden, a bay tree forms part of the garden hedge and is clipped with the privet. It is very healthy.

Overall, the most successful method is growing in a reasonably large pot (say 18"/45 cm diameter) in a warm spot protected from winter winds. Cold wind can damage the leaves, but there will often be new growth from the bottom of the plant the following spring.

To ensure continuous supplies, if you are not sure of hardiness of your plant, take cuttings (as above). Bay is remarkably easy to propagate.

If you are into exotic cookery, you will need some of the more delicate herbs, such as dill, coriander or lemongrass. These will not grow well outdoors unless you live in a really warm area such as Florida or Italy, and will certainly not overwinter.

In their native countries, they are grown as an annual. The plant produces seed, which spreads and produces new plants next spring, whilst the parent dies back. In cooler climates, it is more difficult to get the plants to seed. So, regrettably, unless you are very lucky, you will have to plant fresh seed each spring.

Dill and coriander like rich, heavyish compost, which needs to be kept moist as the plant grows. They do not like transplanting. So sow the seed where you want it to grow, and thin out the young plants if they are getting crowded.

Lemongrass, on the other hand, likes things hot and moist (humid). In most areas, this means growing it in a greenhouse and keeping the compost and the surrounding area damp. It is worth the effort, but may not be a herb which fits in with everyone's growing lifestyle.

Harvesting

All herbs are best used fresh, so pick leaves or bunches as you need them, through the growing season. If the plant is producing lots of leaves and stems, you can also pick now and keep for later. Even if you are planning to dry them, it is better that the leaves are picked at their freshest.

The easiest way to reserve herbs for future use is by freezing. Pick the leaves in the morning.

> **Allotment tip:**
> **pick any leafy or fruiting crop (where the edible bits are up a stem) in a morning, when the sap is rising up the plant and filling the leaves and fruits. Pick root crops in the late afternoon or evening, when the plant is settling to rest and the sap is dropping back into the roots.**

Gently remove the leaves and put in a small plastic or paper bag. This goes into the quick-freeze compartment of the freezer for a day or two.

When you need the herb, remove as much as you need from the bag, rub gently between the palms to break it up, and then use.

If you have a warmish, airy shed, balcony, cellar or protected outside area, you can try drying the herbs. Pick the leaves on stalks and tie into a bunch. Place the whole bunch in a paper bag with the stalks out of the top, and tie that. Then hang the bags up for about a month. You can check if the herbs are ready by opening the bag and gently rubbing a leaf. If it crumbles, it is ready, so take them out and do all the leaves. Store in a lidded jar for use.

Some herbs may overwinter, particularly indoors, and these are obviously available all the time. You may find they are slightly less aromatic than in the summer, so you will need to use a bit more.

DOWN TO EARTH

CHAPTER SEVEN

Back to Your Roots

CHAPTER
 SEVEN

When talking about growing vegetables, we generally categorise them by which part of the plant we eat. So, our first category, root vegetables, is fairly self-evident. It includes carrots, turnips, swedes, parsnips, beetroot and the onion family, including shallots, leeks and garlic. We also include potatoes – which was probably the first "root" you thought of – although, strictly speaking, they are nodules growing on the plant's roots, rather than the roots themselves.

Small diversion: As illustrated by the great Bob Proctor, there may be some disagreement about turnip. He, like me, grew up eating the fleshy root of the turnip, and feeding the leafy top to the animals. In some southern states of USA, the opposite is done – they eat the leaves and give the roots to the animals, so making the plant a leaf vegetable. But this is my book, so we will have my usage – it's a root!

Root vegetables prefer slightly acidic soil. The degree of acidity is not critical and all it means in practice is DO NOT ADD LIME to the soil before planting. For the most part, a rich, healthy soil or compost without too many big stones will produce a perfectly good crop. (Carrots are a bit more particular, but we will come to them later)

All roots will grow in containers. They will need a soil-based compost or your own mix of soil/home-made garden compost/manure, as you have available.

A good container, if you are looking to produce a family-sized crop of root vegetables, is an old dustbin (metal or plastic). Make a number of holes in the bottom for drainage, and then fill to one-third with "drainage material". Traditionally, this has been stones and gravel, but we have latterly used a more modern alternative – expanded polystyrene (the packaging you get around furniture, computers, etc.) If it is a large lump, break it into hand-sized pieces; if it's the smaller packaging, which looks like pasta, just throw it in. The polystyrene works just as well and has the advantage of being much lighter.

> **Tip:**
> **even using polystyrene, a dustbin, filled and planted up, will still be a fair weight, so put it in place before you fill it, to save your back.**

Then simply fill with your chosen soil, gently pressing it down to prevent air pockets, and sow seed or plant plantlets into it.

We will explore individual container needs for each type of vegetable in its section, but a general rule of thumb is to use a container at least 10"/25 cm deep for most roots. If you want longer parsnips, use deeper pots or lengths of piping (drainpipe is ideal).

Potatoes

The old wisdom decreed that potatoes should be planted in new ground (or newly used ground) to break it up. Modern thinking tends to dismiss much of this and puts the effect on the soil down to the gardener earthing up (see chapter 3 and later in this chapter) as the plant grows and lifting the crop at harvest time.

Personally, I don't know which (if either) is actually right. When I started growing, I did it the old way, because that's how I was taught. So that works for me; and it does break up the soil and make it better textured, better textured, so that suits me, too. But you may find that your soil is already fairly loose textured, so the other vegetables will be OK, or you don't want to commit the entire plot to potatoes and you want to grow a range. Well, go for it!

Potatoes like rich soil, lots of food, light and sufficient water. They do not like lime, frost, drying out or being waterlogged. Other than that, they are a most obliging vegetable.

Buying quality, registered, organic "seed" is particularly important with potatoes. Seed, in this case are very small potatoes; they should be bought from a reputable source, although, in future years, you may be able to use your own, if you have stored them correctly. (In reality, you will probably eat all your own crop, because they taste so good).

Seed potatoes are classified as "early", "maincrop" or "late", referring to when they are ready for lifting. What we tend to call new potatoes are usually earlies (or early-lifted maincrop); maincrop takes you through the summer and well into autumn and stores well; lates get you into the winter in storage.

(Yes, you can plant any old bought potatoes which are starting to sprout, but bear in mind that you may not know what type they are and that the crop may not be very big – but, I suppose the seeds are "free".)

So what to plant?

If space is limited or you are growing in pots, plant "earlies" (e.g. "Charlotte", "Duke of York"). In open ground, they can be planted closer together, and in all cases, they grow slightly quicker. The yield may be slightly less than maincrop potatoes, but they will be ready much earlier, and will be less susceptible to disease (see later in this chapter).

If you have enough space or are planting the whole area to start the plot off, plant maincrop varieties such as "Desiree" or "Sante". A perennial favourite is "King Edwards" (sometimes called Red Kings), and these do have a brilliant taste. They are, however, more susceptible to disease and tend to have a lighter yield. I do grow them because the taste is so good, but tend to treat them as earlies (or second-earlies) and put up with the reduced crop.

Whichever type you choose, the process is the same – only the timing varies. Early varieties will be planted out (whether into pots or garden) in early- to mid spring (about April), depending on when the frost has done. Maincrop are planted in late spring/early summer (May). Other than timing, the procedure is much the same for all types.

First, "chit" your potato seeds. This is not as bizarre as it sounds – it just means letting the shoots start growing from the potato. Each "eye" (small, dark, slightly indented patch) on a potato is a potential new shoot. The crop seems to grow better if some of these are already starting to grow when they go into the ground.

To start your seeds off, lay them in a shallow tray or box, with at least one "eye" facing upwards (if possible, the biggest). Put this in a cool, light place and watch the shoots appear. They need to grow until the shoot is about ½"/1½ cm long and a dark purple colour. (If it is longer and green, it is not the end of the world, but get them planted soon, as they are growing a bit too quickly). More than one shoot doesn't matter, so long as they are growing roughly in the same direction.

Once they have got good shoots showing, they are ready to go into the growing space. In the open ground, plant about 12"/30 cm apart and about 4"/10 cm deep, in rows which are about 12"/30 cm apart.

In a 10"/25 cm pot or container, put a layer of drainage material in the bottom and then about 4"/10 cm of soil and compost mixture. This pot will take one moderate seed potato (say about the size to sit in the palm of your hand) in the middle. Cover it with another 4"/10 cm of compost. The level will be well below the rim of the pot – you will see why in a minute.

Wherever you plant, when the green top is about 4"/10 cm tall, you will need to earth up the plant. New potatoes are formed on the upper parts of the roots, so the more roots you can encourage to grow, the bigger the crop. Earthing up covers more of the stem, so more roots grow out sideways from it.

In open ground, pull soil from each side of the row onto the plants to form a mound-and-dip shape (mound around the plants, dip between the rows). On the first earthing up, cover the plant, but on later ones, leave the top few leaves showing. You will need to do this about three times in all.

In containers, just add more soil to give the same effect, until the pot is almost full. Leave about ¾"/2 cm space at the top to prevent the compost washing away and to hold the water.

In the ground, check that no tubers are poking out of the soil. If they do, they will turn green and be inedible, so add some soil to cover them immediately. This is less likely in containers, but the odd tuber may appear at the top. Cover as above.

Other than earthing up, all you now have to do is watch them grow, and water if it is very dry weather (in the UK, this is most unlikely, but you never know!)

The traditional time to lift potatoes is when they begin to flower, but some modern types do not flower. So an alternative check is when the foliage is looking rather droopy and elderly (even though you know they are well watered). Then comes the real treat – lift one or two plants (enough to give sufficient potatoes for a meal) or empty one or two pots. Then all you will need to do is wash the soil off, cook and enjoy. The skins are so thin when the potatoes are this fresh, you will hardly know they are there at all.

Storage

If you have grown lots of early potatoes or your usage hasn't kept up with production, or for maincrops, you will need to store them for future use. The best storage of all is a paper or hessian sack, but a cardboard or wooden box will do as well. The two things you must have is darkness (or they will go green) and coolness. My garden shed, which is in the shady part of the garden, is ideal. It is also helpful to lay a piece of black plastic loosely on the top to ensure dark.

> **Footnote:**
> **Container-grown potatoes will produce a fine, light compost which can be spread around the growing area to help the soil. You can re-use it for some other plants (flowers or herbs, for example), but NEVER re-use it for potatoes or tomatoes (which are a near relative), as any diseases, particularly potato blight, accumulate quite rapidly.**

> **Second footnote:**
>
> Potato blight is a fungus which completely ruins potatoes and tomatoes. It is most likely during damp, warm weather, when it thrives on the leaves of the plants and gets washed down into the roots as well. Early crops rarely suffer, as the weather has not gotten warm enough. Crops can be protected by good earthing up and vigilance. The symptoms are nasty brown blotches on the leaves and the potatoes themselves; as the leaves wither, white, powdery growth forms round the patches.
>
> There is no cure. If you see the signs, dig up the whole plant and destroy it. If the weather is likely to be wet and warm, you can spray with Bordeaux mixture (see appendix 1), which is a reasonable preventative.
>
> Do not plant potatoes or tomatoes in that soil for at least two years.

A bit of more cheerful news – I have never had potato blight in all the years I have grown vegetables. I put this down to healthy soil, crop rotation and always buying quality seed potatoes. So do not get too uptight about it!

Carrots

Carrots do not like stones. The single root (what we call the carrot) will divide to go round any moderate-sized stone it meets, and you will harvest v-shaped vegetables. If the ground is really stony, the root may split a number of times, and your carrot will be three or four thin roots, which are difficult to clean and not much good to eat.

They do not like lots of moisture, either, so a fine, light soil is best of all. The compost used in pots is just right, so carrots grow very well in containers. Dryish growing conditions give sweeter carrots, so good drainage is important, wherever you grow them.

The only real problem is the carrot root fly – a tiny fly which homes in on young carrots, and lays eggs at the base of the stem or just under the soil surface; the young then go downwards and eat the root – your carrot crop. A recent discovery has revolutionised carrot growing. Scientists have found that the root fly never flies higher than about 30"/75 cm above the ground level. Simple solution – grow carrots in a container where the soil level is higher than this. My carrots this year were in pots at the top of a flight of steps – no problem. (An alternative is a tall container such as a dustbin or cleaned out oil drum.)

Previous growers have often grown carrots and onions together. It is believed the scent of the onion puts the carrot fly off the scent of the carrots. This could be complete myth, but I have used it in the past and have suffered no pests when I did.

So prepare your ground. Fill your containers with rich, fine compost. Press down gently, sow the seed on top and cover lightly with more compost (about ½"/¾ cm). If you are growing in open soil, rake it smooth and level, and remove all obvious, largish stones. Run the corner of the rake in a line along the soil to make a shallow dip; sow the seed into this and lightly rake the soil back over them.

In either case, it is best to sow the seed as thinly as you can. This, I know very well, is easier said than done. You nearly always get the seeds unevenly distributed and in small clumps, however hard you try. An allotment tip is to to mix the carrot seed with radish seed and sow them together. The radishes grow much quicker than the carrot and can be pulled up to eat whilst the carrot plants are still small. This will leave natural gaps for the carrots to fill as they grow (it saves thinning, too).

Where you have a number of carrots growing closely together, you will need to thin out the crop as they grow. When the tops are about 3"/8 cm high, pull out every other one to leave some space for the rest to grow. You may have to do this a couple of times. Apart from the first time, when they may be very small, you can probably eat the thinning whole, as salad carrots (they are actually delicious eaten raw!).

A guideline for container growing: if you are planting a standard type of carrot, say "Nantes", you will need a fairly deep pot; the 12"/30 cm "long tom" pot (see chapter 3) is ideal. The "Chantenay", which is rounder and stubbier, will be fine in a standard plant pot.

If you are really going for quantity, then the dustbin is for you. The added advantage here is that you do not have to bend when thinning out or harvesting.

Any carrots which you have not used as the season has gone along should be harvested before they get too old. If left, they become woody and lose much of their sweetness. Lift (by simply pulling on the leaves) when the orange tops are about 1½"/4 cm across for optimum taste (if you wait that long). Any excess crop can be stored in boxes in the cool, till used. Leave the dirt on – do not wash till you are going to use them – and they will store for longer.

Tip: If you have a real glut – more than you need – leave a few in the soil to flower. The hoverflies love their flowers and hoverflies are a gardener's friend – they eat aphids!

Parsnips

The parsnip is one of the most amenable vegetables in the garden. It is sweet to the taste, can be left in the ground till needed and has vey few pests or diseases.

On the down side, they are slow growing and will occupy the plot for a long time, stopping other crop being planted there. So, if space is at a premium in the vegetable plot, perhaps you will have to rethink; however, containers could be the answer.

Parsnip seed germinates better in the open, so mid- to late spring is the traditional time to plant directly into the ground. You can start them earlier, in the greenhouse or on the window ledge, say in February, and plant them out when the soil begins to warm up, or, if you are growing in pots, once the chance of frost has passed.

A simple way of planting is in a "biodegradable seed module" – what we would call a toilet roll middle. This is a useful system which recycles, adds to the soil when planted out, and prevents root disturbance to the young parsnips. Stand a number of toilet roll tubes in a seed tray or similar shallow container. Fill each one with damp compost and gently push in two parsnip seeds. Keep the compost just damp as the seeds grow. When the weather is suitable and the ground is warmed up, simply transfer the whole tube into the final growing site, whether it is open ground or container. In time, the tube will rot down and go into the soil and the roots of the plants will have a bit of protection as they grow.

In open ground, you can sow parsnip with radish (as with carrots), and pick the radish early as a thinner. You may still have to thin out the young radishes to allow parsnips to expand as they grow. Aim for the mature plants to be about 4"/10cm apart. The tube-planted parsnips can be spaced when planted out , and the skinnier plants can be thinned out as they grow.

When growing in containers, allow parsnips a reasonable root space – they grow much longer than carrots. "long tom" pots are ideal and will take three cardboard tubes easily in a 12"/30 cm pot. A 24"/60 cm ornamental container will grow a good crop of about fifteen to eighteen parsnips; and the dustbin will give you a bumper crop.

Another recycling idea: cut ordinary drainpipe (2½"/6½ cm) into lengths of about 15"/40 cm. Fasten a group of them together for security and stability, and stand in a safe area where they will not be knocked over, preferably in a box or tray to prevent soil loss. Fill each with compost and plant two seeds in each – grow as above.

As mentioned before, parsnips can be left in the soil until you want to use them, so storage space is not critical. In many types of parsnip, the flavour actually improves after exposure to frost, so there is no risk in leaving them outside. The only proviso is that they will get rather "woody" in texture if they get really old, so any which you haven't used by about the end of January should be lifted and stored in a cool dark place. The best conditions for storage is a shallow container of dry sand; lay the roots(unwashed) in the sand, not quite touching.

A special treat if your family like potato crisps/chips, is to make your own parsnip crisps. Peel the parsnip, slice very thinly and fry quickly in deep oil. A fine sprinkling of salt, if you wish, is all they will need. They have to be tried to be believed!

The only pest which you need to watch for is the root fly (like carrots), although parsnips are much less susceptible. If in doubt, make sure the top of the containers is more than 30"/75 cm above ground level.

Turnip/swede

Although turnips and swedes are closely related and taste very similar, they do vary in their growth time and soil requirements. Turnips will tolerate damper conditions and need less sunshine. They can be grown between the rows of peas or beans, as they are planted and mature later in the year. Swedes need more sun and lighter soil, and they take twice as long to grow. So choose the appropriate form for your conditions.

Both types are best grown in open ground. They do not do quite as well in containers, although it might be interesting to experiment if you have a big container available. A large ornamental pot, say 18"/45 cm diameter, could well grow about four to six good-sized roots; a dustbin or oil drum will give you a dozen or so. Either will give you sufficient leaf growth to use as a green vegetable in any case.

If you sow the seed in succession, a few at a time, you will be able to harvest as you need them and leave the rest in the ground to mature. Should you have a glut or not be using them quickly enough, lift and store (unwashed) in sand, like the parsnips, in a cool dry place.
Turnips and swedes have few problems. They may be settled by cabbage root fly (although we think of them as a root, they are part of the *Brassica* [greens] family), and in drier areas may attract the flea beetle.

The first can be stopped from happening by using a barrier round the young stem of the plant, which prevents the fly laying eggs where the stem meets the soil. These barriers are called "collars" and can be bought commercially. But you can easily make your own from old carpet, linoleum, roofing felt or thick cardboard. Simply cut a 6"/15 cm round or square from the chosen material, make a hole in the centre about 1 cm across and cut a slit from one edge to this hole. Then simply open it gently and slip around the stem of the plant so that it fits snugly. Once the root has started to develop visibly, the risk is past and they can be removed if you wish.

Flea beetles (a relatively rare problem in northern climes) do not like damp conditions, so regular watering and damp soil will be sufficient to deter them.

Onions

Onions are probably the most widely used vegetables in cooking. To be really self-sufficient, you will need to dedicate a good proportion of your available space to growing enough onions to take you through the year. But it is still worth growing some for your own satisfaction – and the taste.

The good news is that they do not need to be all grown together. They will grow happily amongst other vegetables, except beans, and amongst the flowers in a border, where they have the added value of (possibly) being a pest repellent. They also do well in containers – a good quantity, grouped in a big pot or trough, is best.

Onions can be grown from seeds or "sets" (very young bulbs, grown from seed the previous season). For beginners and for reasonable results, sets are more secure, disease resistant and *much less work*. On the other hand, they are more expensive, particularly if you buy accredited organic sets.

If you choose to grow from seed, you will need to start them off under cover in midwinter. The critical factor is temperature, so you will need a window ledge or greenhouse where the temperature will not fall below 10°C/50°F to ensure germination. Then follow the directions on the packet, potting on the young plants until they are forming small bulbs. These can be planted out into the garden or container in mid- to late spring; this is also when you would be planting sets.

When you first plant out the sets, you may find that they end up laid on the surface of the soil. When this first happened to me, I thought I was hallucinating – I planted them each day and they were pulled up by the next morning. Three times I planted the things before I worked out what was going on.

Birds, particularly pigeons and blackbirds, seem to think that the tops of the sets are worms or grubs and so pull them out to eat them. When they find they are onions, they just abandon them. So, to save work and allow the onions to actually establish themselves and grow, lightly cover the sets with netting (a length of old net curtain will also work). Once they are established and start showing a green shoot, the birds will lose interest and the netting can be removed. In any case, be sure to remove it once there is definite growth. If the new shoots get through the net, they can be easily damaged when it is removed, which can open up the onion to disease.

Once they are underway, onions can be left to their own devices. Weed gently around them as necessary, taking care not to damage them (the skins are surprisingly fragile). They will not need watering and will actually grow more quickly and be slightly sweeter if left slightly dry.

As they ripen, the onion bulb will stick out from the soil surface and then the tops will start to droop (do not bend them over; let it happen naturally). When you can see that they are a nice, rich colour (tan, deep cream or maroon, depending on which type you have sown), lift them gently with a small fork.

Gently shake off the soil and lay your crop in open trays in an airy place to dry off. They can be stored like this until you need them or, if you have the skill, the stems can be plaited or twisted together into strings to hang up in your store (or kitchen) until used. Then you just cut off an onion as you need it, leaving the stalks fastened together (these can join the compost when all the onions have been used).

Sometimes, in spite of all your care, the onions bolt (see chapter 3) and you have silly little bulbs and large stalks and flower heads. There is little you can do about this, so either pull them out and use the space for another crop or leave them and let them go to seed for the birds to enjoy and, maybe, to collect the seeds for next year's crop.

Variations on the bulb onion are shallots and spring onions (scallions). Shallots are a smaller form of the standard onion and can be used in just the same way. They are more commonly used for pickling. They take just the same time to grow as their larger relatives and need the same conditions and treatment. So, unless you are very fond of pickled onions, limited space will probably be better used for standard varieties.

Spring onions/scallions are quite different and great fun to grow. They are classed as salad, and grow quickly and easily, like most salad crops. Grow from seed in the open in either ground or a container. Even if you sow the seed carefully, you will probably have to thin them out as they grow – simply pull out one or two from clumps and let the rest carry on. You can use even the smallest ones in salad or whole in a stir-fry.

A medium pot, say 10"/25 cm, will grow a reasonable crop which will last some weeks, with thinning. It is an ideal crop for children to grow (like most salad) and great fun to watch!

Alternatively, sow the seeds in small clumps amongst the other plants in the salad bed or tub, and pull and use as required.

Garlic

Traditionally, garlic has been considered "foreign" and associated with southern European countries. With the increased use of it in cookery, and a wider knowledge and appreciation of its medicinal qualities (very useful for the heart and blood pressure), it is appearing much more often in vegetable plots, allotments and gardens.

For best results, garlic needs a good cold spell at the beginning and then relative dryness as it matures. So, it is usually planted in late autumn or winter to catch the chill. Its spring and summer state should be sunny and well-drained.

Garlic adapts well to a pot or container, where you can ensure there is good drainage with no chance of water-logging. If you choose to plant in open ground and your soil is inclined to be heavy, add plenty of grit to lighten it and, perhaps, put a small handful of grit underneath each clove of garlic as you plant it.

Each bulb of garlic consists of a number of cloves and each one can produce a new plant. It is just possible to grow on from shop-bought garlic (they will start to sprout if stored long enough), but the growth can be disappointing, as the bulbs are often too old. It is better to buy proper growing bulbs from a reputable source – and the French varieties are some of the best. There are specialist growers, too, such as can be found at www.thegarlicfarm.co.uk.

When you plant your garlic clove, always plant it with the flat base downwards. This may sound self-evident, but garlic is really very fussy about which way it points. Plant about 4"/10 cm deep for best results.

Routine care for garlic is very much like onions, and it enjoys the same sort of conditions. As soon as the leaves begin to fade and turn yellow, it is time to harvest (usually early- to mid summer). Do not be tempted to leave them in the soil, as this will cause resprouting and disease later. Lift them, lay them out to dry well and then store like onions.

Leeks

Unless you belong to the competitive leek growers fraternity and aim to produce to a size and standard needed in a competition, leeks are really easy to grow, unfussy and do not take up very much room. They are a hardy winter vegetable and will grow almost anywhere. They only dislike hot, dry conditions.

Leeks are best grown in open ground. They can be grown in containers which are deep enough (e.g. long tom pots or a deep ornamental container), but the results are never quite as good. They need fairly rich soil, but should not be waterlogged. They can be grown alongside carrots or celery and will help deter carrot fly.

Some leeks are started early under glass in midwinter, and are easier to handle if grown in "modules" (one seed to a module). The simplest module is a toilet roll middle filled with compost. Put them together in a shallow tray on a window ledge or in the greenhouse (it does not have to be heated), water gently and keep the compost just moist as they grow. Alternatively, if your window ledge is already full, plant outdoors in modules, in early spring.

Whichever start you choose, they are usually ready for transplanting when they are about 8″/20 cm tall. If you started them off indoors, they should be "hardened off" first (see chapter 3).

When transplanting, usually in late spring, into their growing position, they must be planted deeply. Make a deep hole with a dibber or piece of broom handle (or similar), about 6″/15cm deep, and drop one plant into it. Then simply fill the hole with water –there is no need to fill with soil, the plant will do all it needs for itself.

Basic maintenance is equally easy – keep free of weeds, and water in dry weather. It may help to give them a feed of dilute seaweed solution or a top-dressing of sulphate of ammonia (see appendix 1) in late summer, particularly if they are in a container, but this is not essential if the soil is good.

To get longer white stems, pull earth round the stem (earthing up) as they grow, being careful not to get it inside the growing leaves.
Lift leeks as you want to use them. They will happily stay in the ground until needed and are not troubled by frost or cold once they are grown.

DOWN TO EARTH

CHAPTER EIGHT

Social Climbers: Peas and Beans

CHAPTER
 EIGHT

The showing-off name for this group of crops is *legumes*. It includes peas, runner (stick) beans, French (kidney) beans, dwarf beans, broad beans, butter (fava) beans and asparagus (yard long) beans. All legumes are grown as annuals, and fresh seed is planted each spring (you can save some of your own if you have enough). Generally, we eat the seeds and seed pods, which can be fresh, dried, or frozen.

Legumes are called nitrogen-fixers because they store nitrogen (a useful growing chemical) in little nodules on the roots. This then goes back into the soil when the plant dies. This is quite unusual, as most plants simply take nitrogen out.

Although they need similar basic growing conditions, peas and beans can vary considerably in their needs and, particularly, in the weather conditions they like.

Legumes are all greedy plants and need plenty of richness in their soil. It isn't possible to over-manure the area where you are going to plant them – they will take all you can give them. You can even manure under the space immediately before planting the seeds, with almost anything (other than brand-new farm manure, which is still a bit too strong).

One tip is to dig a shallow trench along the planting line and put a load of compost or similar into it – you can even add shredded paper, household waste or grass clippings. Cover with soil, then plant the seeds above it.

All peas and beans are affected by the same pests and disease, so they should not be planted in the same soil every year (see crop rotation, chapter 3). They all need sunshine, and some – particularly French and dwarf beans – need a reasonable amount of warmth, so they may not be as successful in more northern areas.

Legumes grow quite happily in groups, block or circles (see runner beans), except peas – these are much happier in a straight line. That said, I have grown all types in both lines and blocks and had quite acceptable results.

Many types need some sort of support whilst growing, or they will end up as a tangle on the ground, smothering each other. In many cases, the support need only be minimal and about 2'/50 cm high. However, some runner beans get very tall, and you will have to prepare substantial support as you plant them. It will be too late if you wait till they are half-grown; they will have colonised the ground, and it is very difficult to persuade them to go upwards then.

Sowing

Most pea and bean seeds are sown directly into the growing space, once the weather starts to warm up. There is no point sowing early to get early crops – they won't germinate if the soil is cold, and the seeds will rot, so they will not germinate later, either.

The only way to bring them on early is under cover, in an unheated greenhouse or cold frame. Indoors, the central heating may be too much, so the spare bedroom window ledge or a light, unheated porch is probably your best bet.

Seeds are best sown in modules, with one seed to each section, to avoid root disturbance later. Reusing plant trays (the sort which hold six small plants or similar) is ideal or you can resort to our old favourite, the toilet roll middle.

If you are intending to plant out into an open patch of ground, an allotment ruse is to plant your seeds in a length of old plastic guttering. Just fill with compost and plant the seeds about 6"/15 cm apart along its length. When the plants are ready to go outside, make a shallow trench the same length as the guttering, and carefully slide the whole contents, soil and plants, sideways into the trench. Firm gently in its new space, and water in to grow.

However you plant, the supports should be put in place at the same time. In the case of runner beans, put the supports in place first, as this will involve a certain amount of walking on the area. You can then loosen the soil as you plant.

Support

Different legumes have different growing habits, so the support needed will reflect this. Peas climb by sending out tendrils which curl round other bits of plants (e.g. twigs or leaves). This gives support and purchase to the growing stem.

One of easiest forms of support for peas is netting, draped over a frame of canes or pieces of wood. Some growers prefer to use metal chicken fencing, as this is a little more stable. The cheapest (free) method is to use woody twigs. You can collect these from local woods or anyone who has been pruning a tree or shrub. You will need pieces about 3'/90 cm long, with a few branches or twigs (rather than a single stem). Push one for each seed into the ground, so it looks like a small hedge.

Runner and French beans, however, twine the whole stem around their chosen support. They will be content with a single stick for each plant. The most common supports are bamboo canes, which will last for many years and can be reused over again. If you have somewhere to anchor the ends, you can use heavy-duty string or wire attached at each end. But, they will be taking a lot of weight by the time the plants are fully grown, so you must be sure that they will stay anchored.

The canes can be arranged in pairs in two rows, crossing at the top and tied together firmly. When you have completed the row, lay other canes along the top joins for stability. Or put your canes in a ring and bring them all together like wigwam. This is particularly good for on top of a large container.

Lastly, use what you have – remember Norman's spiral staircase (chapter 4)?

Broad beans and white beans are not natural climbers. Some of the smaller varieties will actually stand quite well unsupported, but the standard varieties need something, or they will bend with the wind. A simple system is a number of canes or robust sticks along the row with string or wires running between them. As the beans grow, you tuck the stems around the wires, and this will be sufficient support.

Containers

Although peas are happier growing in open ground, all legumes will actually grow in containers. Beans, in particular, like pots, as the pots themselves absorb heat from the sun, and, so, increase the warmth factor to the crop; and because containers have really good drainage, there is less risk of waterlogging.

Even if you are using good quality potting compost, it is helpful to add some manure or garden compost to the mix when you fill the pots, just as you would in open ground planting. As with most container growing, do ensure that there is a good layer of crock, stones or polystyrene lumps in the bottom for drainage. This should be about 4"/10 cm deep.

If the weather is particularly wet, or you can see that the soil in the pot is staying very wet, lift the pot up a little by putting pot feet (bought) or a few lumps of stone, brick or block (free) under the pot to raise it off the ground a little (at least high enough to slide your hand underneath).

For standard runner (stick) beans, you will need quite a large container – a 30"/75 cm ornamental pot is ideal (this gives you about 15"/38 cm depth of soil). In such a pot, sow four seeds or young plants around the edge. Put a long cane (5'/1.5 m at least) behind each, pushed well in to the soil. Fasten them all together at the top, to form a wigwam; unless you get extremely strong gales, they will support each other and the fully grown bean plants quite well.

Dwarf/French beans can cope with a smaller container, or you can put more in the size of pot you used for the runners (say, six to eight plants, instead of four). Also, the supports need not be quite so tall, although you will still need something. If you haven't enough support canes or sticks, you can avoid support altogether by making the plants grow as a bush instead. This involves "pinching out": when the plant is about 1'/30 cm high, gently break off the very top of the main shoot (called pinching out because the easiest way is to nip it between thumb and first finger).

Pinching out stops the plant growing temporarily (you have removed the "growing tip"). So then it produces new shoots to carry on – usually two, one each side of where you pinched out. When these are 8"/20 cm high, pinch them out, too. The plant will repeat the process and produce more side shoots

Pinch these out when they get to a sufficient size, and you are well on the way to producing a bush effect with the plant; three times should be enough to produce a reasonable sized bush. Then, let it grow and produce a crop in the normal way.

Peas, because they like to be in rows, are very happy in troughs or "Grobags" (though you can use pots if that is all you have). Wooden fruit boxes, lined with old plastic bags (with holes in them for drainage), old plastic sacks or bin bags tied at the open end and slit along the length (our dog food sacks are ideal for this, being pretty robust), old drawers or bookshelves lined with plastic: all can be adapted to planting. See what you can scrounge from your shed (or your neighbours'- with their permission, of course!).

Yields

On average, a runner bean plant will provide about 1 lb/½ kilo of beans, although, in my garden, I get rather more than that. So, for an average family (2 adults plus 2.4 children), if you are not to get sick of eating beans, ten plants will give you fresh pickings through the summer and leave some to freeze for later in the year.

Runner beans are the heaviest croppers in the legume family. French or dwarf beans will provide about ¾ lb/0.4 k for each plant; broad beans and peas will give about ½ lb/0.2 k for each plant.

Companions

Most legumes cohabit quite happily with other crops. The only problem is that fully grown peas and beans create fairly heavy shade, so any crops growing between them are starved of light (particularly between runner beans, which are very dense once they are mature).

However, you can use the ends of the growing period effectively. You can sow early salad crops (lettuce, radish, spring onions) at about the same time as the peas and beans. They will get a bit of protection from the taller peas as they grow and will be picked and eaten before the peas or beans get too big.

Towards the end of the legume growing season, plant your winter greens as the peas and beans are coming to an end and starting to die back. They will benefit from the nitrogen from the peas' roots and will carry on growing after the peas have gone.

Broad beans are the earliest legumes and can be planted with the seed potatoes. They will give some protection to the young potato plants, in case there is a late frost.

Peas

Peas are possibly the most fiddly of the legumes to grow, and need slightly richer soil than the beans. But they are still not difficult, and the taste of freshly picked peas is one of the summer's greatest pleasures – well worth the effort.

Peas are best started off under cover if possible and planted out when the soil is warming up (see chapter 6 – check the hedges). Apart from anything else, this will protect the seeds from theft. Yes, there are seed thieves! Not human – birds and mice; both love pea seeds. (Early on in my gardening career, I used most of a packet of pea seeds before I realised why no plants were coming up. The pigeons were just waiting for me go indoors and then snaffling the lot!)

If you have to plant straight outdoors, give the seeds some protection by covering with netting (open ground or containers) until the young plants are about 2–3″/5–8 cm high. Then the netting can be removed without damaging the plants and they will grow on from there.

There are some varieties of dwarf pea which do not need as much (if any) support, but generally these tend to crop much less than the older standard types. If you are to get the maximum food from your patch, choose a standard variety (say, any of the "Kelvedon" range), and give them support (see above).

The one area where peas are particularly sensitive is water. Once you have planted out the young plants and watered them in, you can largely leave them alone, unless there is a sudden drought and they are wilting (most unlikely in a British spring). Too much water at this stage will just encourage the growth of leaves rather than flowers (it is flowers which will produce the pods, so the more the merrier). Once the plants are flowering, water if the weather is dry. Also, when the pods start to swell (there are seeds growing inside), keep fairly well watered, to help swell the crop.

Regular weeding is useful, as weeds will take up nutrients and water which the peas need. When the plants are young, weeds may also strangle the weaker pea plants, so it is common sense to give the crop every chance that's available.

It is unlikely that an average garden will be able to produce more peas than you can cope with, but if you can, they will freeze very well. Unpod the peas, lay them on a shallow tray and put into the quick-freeze section. Do not wash before freezing – this slows down the process – you can wash them before cooking. When they are frozen, shake them into a bag and store till needed.

But the real pleasure is fresh, newly picked garden peas. There is no taste

taste quite like them. Your only problem may be stopping the family eating them raw before you can get them to the dinner table!

Runner beans

Of all the legumes, runner/stick/climbing beans give the best value for money. The old varieties, in particular, give a good crop, and you do not need a large number of plants. They will grow in most soils and containers and amongst other plants or flowers. And they are quite pretty!

On the downside, they do grow very tall and quite thick, so will create shade to nearby plants. They are best grown at the back of a sunny border, against a wall or in an area where there will be nothing growing immediately behind them. They will need sun to grow, so a sunny back corner is ideal.

Beans are sensitive to frost and cold, so do not plant out your young plants or sow seed until you are sure the frosts are over. NB. If you are caught out by a really late frost and it kills the young plants or stops the seeds from germinating, do not despair. Wait a week or so and replant. Although the seeds are starting later, they will catch up as the weather warms, and your final crop won't be that much later. In fact, some gardeners plant half their crop in late spring and half in early summer, which gives them beans right through to the autumn.

The young plants are much enjoyed by slugs and snails, so give them some protection with a plastic bottle cloche over each one. By the time they have reached the neck of the bottle, they should be relatively safe. (You may find the odd leaf nibbled at the bottom of the plant, but this should not be sufficient damage to threaten it).

All runner beans need support, which should be big enough to take the full-sized plant. Remember, a fully grown, standard bean can reach 6'/1.8 m, and will be quite heavy when full of leaf and beans. Bamboo canes are a good .

support – just make sure they are long enough. If you live near a wood, you may be able to collect sapling branches to use as supports.

Once the plants are underway, they will twist up the support quite happily. They will need little care other than watering in dry weather. This is particularly important when the flowers appear. Sometimes you will get plenty of flowers but few pods forming – this is almost always because of lack of water. So water daily, in the evening for preference, if it doesn't actually rain. Also, water thoroughly. These are big plants, and they want a good, heavy drink. Let the hose run along the roots until the soil is really wet, rather than just a drop to damp the surface. Yes, it is a lot of work, but it will pay off when you harvest a bumper crop of beans.

When the plant has almost reached the top of the support, pinch out the tip. This will stop major growth, although it may get a bit higher from lower growth. Also it will encourage growth from lower down the stem, which puts the weight lower down and stops the plant from being top-heavy.

Once you have a crop growing, pick regularly, whilst the beans are not too big. They will be sweeter and crisper (older pods get a bit rubbery). Picking also encourages more flowers to form higher up the stalk and so provides you with more beans.

If you do get a glut or you get fed up of eating them, they freeze very well, either whole or sliced. A few pods can be left on the plants for seed for the next year. Leave them on the plant until they begin to look brown and old (but before they pop open). Open the pods and remove the seeds, and lay them in a shallow tray in a warmish place to finish drying out – NOT in the sun, which will cook them. Once dry, store in a paper bag or cardboard box in a dark, dry, cool place till next spring.

French (dwarf) beans

In many ways, French beans seem to be just miniature runner beans, but the taste and habit will tell you that they are a different type.

For a start, they need much more warmth than runner beans. There are areas which are generally too cold at the ends of the growing season – the seeds cannot be planted until the soil is really warmed up, and the cold stops the pods from ripening at the end of the season. So, the growing period is too short for an effective crop. That said, if you have a sun-trap part of your patch, or live in a mild area, French beans are a most rewarding crop.

The easiest French beans to grow are the "bush" varieties (e.g. "the Prince"). They do take up as much space and only need low support – say 3'/1 m canes or bean sticks. They can be planted in rows, blocks or rings, with the canes making a wigwam (like the runners).

BUT, whether you choose bush plants or the taller climbing varieties, they cannot be planted out until the soil is really warm. Plant too early, and you will simply waste your seeds (if sowing directly into the soil) or kill off the young plants you have been nurturing.

You can help the warming up process by covering the soil with cloches or spreading clear plastic film over it. This will need to be done for several weeks prior to planting out. You can plant seed from early summer onwards directly into the soil or transplant seedlings which you started earlier in the greenhouse. If you are at all unsure about temperature, cover each baby plant with a plastic bottle cloche until they start to grow vigorously (probably a week or two).

Like most beans, care is relatively simple. They need plenty of water, so this is another daily task, unless it has rained properly. Keep the area free of weeds. A heavy mulch of garden compost will effectively do both jobs for you, suppressing weeds and conserving water. It will also protect the lower pods from getting dirty from the soil (not essential but aesthetically pleasing). French bean seed is self-fertile, which means that the seed will be identical to the parent. So, you can save the seed for next year's planting. Save in the same way as for runner beans.

Although we have referred to these as French beans, you may come across alternative names. If they are grown to maturity and then dried for storage, they are called "haricot" beans (and can become baked beans); if they are picked when half ripe and quite small, they are "flageolets" and are shelled and eaten like peas.

Whatever your choice, French beans are good croppers, freeze very well as either shelled beans or the whole pods, and are probably one of the tastiest things you will ever grow.

Broad beans

Among my acquaintances, I find opinion is sharply divided about broad beans. People seem to either love them or hate them – no middle ground. If you know you hate them, pass on to the next section and keep your growing plot for something else. If you have never tried them, read on – it's worth trying anything once!

Broad beans are the largest and earliest of this botanical family. They can be planted out in the autumn for an early crop in the spring, or in early spring for summer harvesting. They generally do not grow too tall and will often not need support (some dwarf types only grow to about 2'/60 cm tall).

Unlike most beans, they are not quite so light-sensitive, so will grow in the slightly shadier areas of your plot or where the sunlight only reaches for part of the day.

Like all beans, broad beans can be planted directly into the soil or raised in modules and planted out as seedlings. To give a succession of crops, aim to plant out the next batch when the first (or previous) lot are about 3"/8 cm tall. Be sure that the soil was well dug previously and is reasonably well drained. Then put in the seeds and away you go. They will need very little attention.

A problem

The one nuisance which is peculiar to broad beans (rather than any other variety) is aphids (black fly). Aphids love the growing tips of broad beans, and it is not unusual to have normal plants one day and totally black-covered tops the next. If the aphids are not removed, they will eat into the stem and seriously weaken the plant and your crops.

There are few organic sprays available, although some growers use warm, soapy water very successfully. The young plants will need to be sprayed each week as they grow, from about 1'/30 cm tall. Make sure that the growing tip is particularly wet.

(When I was growing up and learning gardening, the allotment owners used a nicotine spray, which they made themselves. Most were pipe smokers, and used a small amount of tobacco, boiled up, strained and then diluted for use. The smell of the boiling is a sharp and acrid memory! This spray did work – it was most effective against aphid. You must decide if you wish to go down that route. It is an organic solution, but nicotine is not exactly a popular commodity.)

If you are not particularly squeamish, it is easy enough to run your fingers along the tip of each plant, squashing the aphids as you go. It doesn't look nice, but it is effective.

In an established garden, you may have sufficient hoverflies and similar predators, which will relish the feast of aphid, but until you have the balance, the control will be up to you.

Harvest

All peas and beans freeze well, so any surplus can be stored for later use. Peas, French beans and broad beans can go straight into the quick-freeze section on trays and then be bagged up when frozen. Do not wash them at this stage – they freeze better, with less external damage, if they are dry. You can always wash them before cooking.

For runner beans, I personally prefer to slice them, then blanch, dry and freeze in single portion bags. But it is not critical, and they can be frozen whole if you prefer.

After the harvest

As we said at the beginning of this chapter, legumes are "nitrogen fixers" – they put nitrogen back into the soil when they die back. To make sure this happens, you must leave the roots in the soil to die back naturally and release the nitrogen, which they have stored.

So, after you have picked the crop of peas or beans and the plant is beginning to look rather sad, do not pull them up for the compost heap, as we do with most plants. Cut the plants off about 4"/10cm from ground

ground level. All the cut off tops can go into the compost, but leave the roots where they are. If you can leave them for a week or two, that is ideal, but if your space is limited and you need to plant the next crop, simply dig the roots in gently and plant in the normal way. The new crops will not suffer.

The crops to benefit most from the nitrogen fixing are *Brassica*s (greens). They are greedy nitrogen users. So, if your programme allows, plant your greens where the legumes were and increase your winter yield, as well.

CHAPTER  NINE

Being Greens

CHAPTER

NINE

If people were asked about childhood food, most of them would have horrible memories about being made to eat cabbage (or similar green vegetables). "Eat up your greens, they're good for you," seems to have been a haunting childhood mantra. It is, therefore, not surprising that few adults appreciate the value and variety of green vegetables – the *Brassica* family.

This range of vegetables, as the name suggests, is grown for its leaves. As well as the dreaded cabbage, the group includes cauliflower, sprouts, kale, broccoli and spinach. They come in a variety of shapes, colours and sizes, but all have similar properties.

Form the nutritional point of view, mother was right – greens are good for you! As a vegetable group, they probably have the best vitamin- and trace element content of anything you can grow. Virtually all greens contain vitamins A, B6, C, and E, plus calcium, magnesium and some potassium, and most (though, surprisingly, not spinach – despite Popeye's claims!) contain some iron. All greens contain high quantities of phytochemicals – powerful anti-cancer antioxidants.

So, for your health, make room in your garden for greens, if you can. From a purely aesthetic viewpoint, *Brassicas* can be surprisingly attractive. Although known as greens, the greens can vary from the yellow and red stalks of Swiss chard to the bottle green of savoy cabbage. Red can be scarlet, as in the stalks of kale, to the maroon of red cabbage. It is worth experimenting with varieties for interesting growing areas.

The downside of *Brassica*s is that they have a long growing period. Most are in their growing area by late spring and will not be harvested until autumn or early winter. If your space is limited, this may not be an efficient use of it.

There is also the size of some plants. Even if you are not planning to grow giant vegetables, cabbage and cauliflower still occupy a goodly space. Each plant can be 1'/30 cm across, including the outer leaves.
On the plus side, they can be left in the ground until needed for eating. Cabbage and broccoli can give you two good crops: by cutting out the middle of the plant in summer, and leaving the outer leaves in place, it will produce a second growing for cutting later.

All *Brassica*s tolerate partial shade and do not mind damp soil. The plants covered in this section are all at home in the cooler, damper conditions of northern countries. There are oriental members of the *Brassica* family (pak choi, komatsuma), but they are rather more specialist in their growing needs.

*Brassica*s benefit from water-retentive, fertile soil which is not too light in texture. If your soil is sandy, add plenty of organic matter well in advance of planting.

As a rule, always grow your *Brassica*s from seed. Unless you know exactly where and how they are grown, do not buy plants to transplant into your own garden. It is too easy to bring in the clubroot disease, and once that is in your plot, it can stay for up to twenty years and ruin all future *Brassica* crops (see special section at the end of the chapter).

Crop rotation is an automatic part of organic growing, and it is especially beneficial to greens. Grow them in the area, or compost, if in a container, where your peas or beans had ben before. They will benefit from the extra nitrogen left in the soil by the peas.

Because of the space they need, if you are growing in containers, you will have to allocate good-sized ones. Generally, cabbage, cauliflower and broccoli need a bucket-sized container for each plant, although you can get three broccoli plants in a 3'/90 cm diameter tub.

Whatever the container, the compost must be very rich. Ideally, mix rich potting compost and farmyard manure or garden compost in equal proportions. Firm it down in the container before planting, to avoid looseness.

During growing, water becomes very important (even more than most container-grown plants). Be prepared to water very regularly in dry weather.

Sowing

You can start *Brassica* seeds indoors, if you have the space, or in a greenhouse or similar, and this will mean that the crop will be ready a bit earlier. It's not the end of the world if you can't – so follow the packet instructions for sowing straight outdoors. If you have started them off under cover, here is an allotment tip for planting them out into the final growing space: Plant out on a dull, preferably showery day. This seems to settle the young plants in without stress. If it is too sunny, they will tend to wilt and then have to work harder, just to survive.

When you plant any *Brassica*, firm the soil around the young plant. If your soil is very light, use your heel to give the firming some power. It is better to have the ground over-firm rather than over-soft.

Young *Brassica* plants are very popular with the birds – they will peck the young leaves almost to extinction. So give them some protection by with netting until they are established. Protect against root fly by planting through growing fleece or using collars (see later section).

Soil tips

- **If soil is light or sandy, plant out each plant surrounded by a shallow dip; then fill the dip with rich organic matter as the plant grows.**
- **If the soil is clay or heavy, plant on level ground and gently earth up round the stem as it grows (this helps to prevent waterlogged roots).**

Companions

*Brassica*s will grow happily with peas. They can be planted between the rows of pea plants and will grow slowly in the partial shade, until the peas are harvested, when they will take over the area. If you are growing peas in a tub, plant the peas around the outside, and a cabbage or cauliflower can go in the middle.

It is believed that there is a benefit from growing them with herbs such as chamomile, dill, sage or rosemary. Possibly, the smell from the herbs deters the cabbage white butterfly – certainly, older growers of my acquaintance swear by them.

*Brassica*s will also cohabit happily with potatoes, celery and onions, but do not plant near runner beans, lettuce or strawberries.

In a mixed bed, or if you are infilling in a general flower border, *Brassica*s will grow amongst most garden flowers, except the acid-loving ones. So, do not plant near camellias, azaleas, rhododendrons or heathers.

Cabbage

The best known, and probably most misused, *Brassica* is the cabbage. If your strongest memory is of a dollop of pale green, overcooked, damp shredded leaves, the dislike of the cabbage is hardly surprising. But it has so much to offer for growing and eating fresh from the garden.

Varieties range from the (usually) dark green spring cabbage – they look like a bunch of leaves fastened together – through the pointy-topped summer varieties, to the solid, round white or deep red winter cabbage. You can take in dark, curly edged savoy types (a sharper, more peppery taste) or the almost white "coleslaw", on the way. It is possible to plant a cabbage for each part of the year.

Whichever you choose, plant into moist, firm soil and make sure the young plants are kept moist for the first few weeks. Once established, they are much less fussy and need relatively little care. In containers, you may have to monitor them a little more closely, as they will dry out more readily than in open ground. If the leaves are looking a bit limp and droopy, water well. Better still, keep the soil in the container moist all the time.

The cabbage white butterfly is a delightful-looking creature which will wreck your crop if allowed. Watch out for its eggs or caterpillars on your plants. Probably the first thing you will notice will be holes appearing in the outer leaves. If there are only a few, the plant can probably tolerate them, but too many will eat the entire cabbage. The surest control is to pick them off or squash them by hand (Yes, it is gooey, but it's effective. Wearing rubber gloves can help!). Alternatively, keep your cabbages under growing fleece to prevent the butterflies getting to them.

Brussels sprouts

Sprouts are really little cabbages, growing from a single main stem. Again, a much maligned vegetable, due mainly to being eaten when old and overcooked (most people have experienced the Christmas obligation!). If grown well and picked young, sprouts can be as delicate and sweet a green vegetable as you can get.

Sprouts grow up a main stem, which can be very thick and tall when mature. Because of this, they do need a good, firm rooting system to anchor them. If they wobble around in the ground too much, it will seriously set back the cropping.

> **Allotment tip:**
> **If your area is very windy, plant your sprouts in threes, so that, when they are mature, they can be tied together at the top. The tripod formed will stand up to the wind much better.**

Fortunately, the cure is fairly simple. First, dig in lots of organic matter, particularly if your soil is fine or sandy, well in advance of planting out. In a container, make sure that at least half the soil is rich garden compost or manure. Then, when you do plant out, firm the soil round each young plant thoroughly with your heel. This might seem drastic round such a small, young plant, but it will pay off with time.

Sprouts prefer planting in open ground, but they will grow in containers, although the crop might be lessened. The containers must be deep enough. For a single plant, a bucket is ideal; for three plants together you would need a big container (e.g. a dustbin or a 2½'/75 cm ornamental pot). Whichever you choose, firm down the soil/compost very firmly, both when you are filling and as you plant the young sprouts.

Cauliflower

Although popular to eat, cauliflowers are not the easiest vegetable to grow. The cauliflower is a hybrid version of broccoli, which produces a large, white, multi-flowered head, rather than the looser green heads.

So, first of all, what are you up against?

1. Cauliflower requires really rich, moist, heavy soil. If your soil is light or sandy, forget it. You will only reap frustration.

2. They need consistent watering or the florets will grow deformed or weedy. Even a UK summer will not provide enough water to keep the soil moist enough, so you must be willing to water almost every day it does not rain.

3. They need lots of room. Each plant will need about 1–2'/50 cm square of space (there are some slightly smaller varieties which can grow closer together). Also, they will occupy that space right through the summer and autumn.

4. Planting times can be critical, both for sowing seed and planting out young plants. So read the seed packet carefully. Plant out the seedlings as soon as possible, once they are hardened off, if starting them under cover.

So why bother? If you have the space, time and patience, the end result is very rewarding and great to eat. If you can successfully grow cauliflower, you have come of age as a gardener. Give yourself a reward and permit yourself to be smug for a day or two!

On a positive note, cauliflower can be grown in a container, if it is sufficiently large. As with cabbage, you will need at least a bucket-sized pot for each plant. The growing compost must be very rich and heavy with lots of organic content. Most importantly you must be prepared to water – do not let the compost dry out.

Kale

Of all the *Brassica*s, kale is probably the easiest to grow and the most reliable for the beginner. It is hardy and gives fresh greens right through the winter.

Like all the other *Brassica*s, kale needs rich soil, but it does not like being waterlogged. So, once you have established the young plants, they need relatively little care and far less watering than other greens.

Kale is picked leaf by leaf, as it matures and as you need it. This gives it a "pick and come again" habit – if picked regularly, it will produce new leaves through the season. So, although each plant needs a moderate amount of space (about 1–1½'/30–45 cm), you can produce enough leaves to feed you through the season from as few as six plants.

Kale is an ideal crop for containers, where the drainage is a definite asset to growing. A good sized pot (say 12"/30 cm) will take a single plant; or put a group together in a big ornamental container. As always, the soil must be very rich and heavy, but you will only have to water during times of drought, rather than every day it doesn't rain.

There are a number of dwarf varieties of kale, which are particularly suitable for small gardens or growing areas. They can look very attractive planted amongst the flower beds, and the curly leaves make a good contrast

contrast to the coloured stalks. Dwarf varieties are also less likely to be blown over in winter gales, but to be on the safe side, put your containers where they can get some shelter from strong winds.

Sprouting broccoli (calabrese)

The best known variety is the purple sprouting broccoli. There is also a white form, but this is much less hardy and produces a noticeably smaller crop. Calabrese is an Italian version, which is becoming very popular with both growers and eaters.

Although the traditional purple broccoli has a more delicate and sweet flavour, it is a fact that calabrese is very pleasant and very much easier for the novice grower. Usefully, it also takes up less space and grows quicker.

Neither variety transplants very well, so it is best to sow the seed directly where it will be growing. This can be in open ground, the flower beds or a container. As for all *Brassica*s, the soil should be very rich and moisture-retentive. Like kale, calabrese and broccoli do not like being waterlogged, so they do grow well in containers. Calabrese will need a 12"/39 cm pot for each plant, but broccoli needs at least an 18"/45 cm one.

Having sown both in the spring, calabrese will be ready for harvest by autumn, but the sprouting broccoli will be pickable in winter, and, possibly, through until the spring. If, instead of pulling up the whole plant, you cut the main head of the calabrese whilst it is fairly young and firm (before the florets start opening away from each other), it will encourage side shoots to form, giving further, though smaller, crops later in the season.

Nasties

*Brassica*s have their fair share of predators and diseases, although new strains are being produced with increased resistance.

Some problems, such as the cabbage white butterfly, can be more of a nuisance than really devastating. A few cabbage white caterpillars will make a mess of the outer leaves of a cabbage, but will not actually kill the plant. Clever planting can help offset this nuisance.

How butterflies (and other insects) taste things

It has been discovered that insects taste plants they land on, to see if they are suitable food for their young. They do this through their feet. But, to be sure the plants are right, they take at least four samples – they flit from plant to plant, tasting, and when all four taste the same, they lay their eggs. If they do not get a repeat taste, they go away to the next group of plants. So, planting in rows gives the insect a line to follow and a succession of identical plants (a bit like a green runway). Alternatively, plant in blocks, rather than rows, and next to a block of something different. The insect will not get a proper taste and will look elsewhere

---

But there are two nuisances peculiar to *Brassica*s which are devastating and should be avoided – the cabbage root fly and clubroot disease.

Cabbage root fly

Exactly as the name suggests, this is a small fly, about 1 cm long, which looks like a housefly. It lays its eggs just below the soil surface, next to the stems of young greens. When the eggs hatch, the maggots point downwards and eat into the plant's roots. The plants, especially young ones, rarely recover, and, if they do, they are spindly and of poor quality.

What to look for

The first and most obvious sign is the plant's leaves wilting and looking slightly bluish. If you pull it up, the roots will be black and rotting.

You may be able to see the eggs around the stem, and these can be removed by hand (rubber gloves again, as they need to be squashed). The plants will probably then grow on. But do not plant greens in that place or that compost/soil for a couple of years, just in case!

How to avoid it

Fortunately, the root fly is a creature of habit. It likes to land on the young plant, walk down the stem until it touches soil, and then turn round and egg-lay. If any part of this routine is prevented, it is confused! So if it cannot lay its eggs exactly as it wants, it will go somewhere else.

The simplest (though not the cheapest) prevention is to stop the fly getting to the plant stem or the soil by covering the crop with horticultural fleece. Be sure to peg it down to prevent flies getting underneath, and raise it as the plant grows until the *Brassica* is about half size, when it should be safe.

A simple, home-made solution is the *Brassica* collar. Cut squares of old carpet, underlay, lino, even very thick cardboard into 6"/15 cm squares. Cut a slit from one side to the middle and widen out the centre a bit to form a rough, small hole:

As you plant each *Brassica*, put a collar around the base of the stem, on the ground (if sowing seed directly in the growing area, add the collar when the plant is about 4"/10 cm tall).

This simple device will prevent the fly getting to the soil and laying its eggs. Even if it does lay eggs on the collar (unlikely), you will see them and can remove them. And, the grubs which do hatch cannot get down the roots to feed, and will die.

If the collars are made from cardboard and you do not want to re-use them, leave them on the ground and they will rot down naturally. Otherwise, remove them when you pick your greens and store them for next year

Club root disease

Club root is a fungal disease, and a considerably more serous problem. It will kill your *Brassica*s and allied plants such as radish, wallflowers and stocks. In suitable conditions, the fungal spores can stay in the soil for many years, so it will affect future crops. Worst of all, there is virtually no cure.

Having doom-mongered, there are many ways to prevent club root getting into your plot in the first place, and all are within anyone's abilities.

What to look for

Initially, the plants will wilt and look sickly. Then the leaves will develop a purple-red tinge. The roots will fuse together or swell into thick galls. Eventually the roots may rot and the plant will die.

How to avoid it

a. Grow *Brassica*s from seed. Only bring in plants from elsewhere if you know they are from a clean source.

b. Lime the soil about 3–6 months before planting out the young greens. Club root likes acidic conditions, so the alkalinity of the lime will offset this. If container growing, this will mean planning ahead and filling the containers and adding lime well ahead – say before Christmas. (Amounts? About a handful of lime will be adequate for a single plant pot, two for a large container with three plants. On open ground, a "dusting" – so it looks like a light frost. You are unlikely to put too much on if you scatter it rather than blob it.)

c. Keep soil free-draining, with plenty of organic matter, compost, etc. The disease spores like the wet. If you have fine, quick-drying soil, or it is a very dry season, there will be little threat.

Tip:
home-made garden compost reduces the risk of attack better than anything

d. Crop rotation is essential. Grow all your *Brassica*s in one area and change it each year. If you are growing in containers or have limited space, change the compost and use the old on the compost heap or for other plants.

> **Tip:**
> **growing amongst leeks seems to be beneficial.**

Good general hygiene will be a major factor in preventing this disease ever arriving in your garden. I have (thank goodness) never experienced it in all my growing years. I put this down to sensible gardening practice and home-made compost.

DOWN TO EARTH

CHAPTER
 TEN

Away You Go: The Gardening Year

CHAPTER
 TEN

Hopefully, by now, you will be keen to start growing something. So, what to start right now? Well, that obviously depends on what time of year it is. Although we have mentioned seed sowing times in a number of sections previously, it might be useful to have a month-by-month list. So, whenever you acquire this book, you can check what you can start doing, right now!

January

This is the easiest month of the year in terms of work – there is hardly any! Nothing can be planted. Even in the mildest of areas, the soil is too cold for starting off plants (those that are already in will have acclimatised by now).

So enjoy yourself reading the seed catalogues and planning what you are going to grow this year and order your seeds.

If you live in a mild area and are planning an early start, you can cover the soil you are going to cultivate to warm it up a little. Black polythene sheet is the traditional cover; make sure it is well anchored, or the winter winds will lift and tear it, which makes it useless (and a mess).

If you already have fruit trees, these can be pruned, whilst they are dormant. The RHS website gives excellent step-by-step guides on pruning.

Otherwise, brush heavy snow off the trees, shrubs and crops, to prevent them breaking, and enjoy the rest.

February

Indoors/greenhouse

Start off the early vegetables, towards the end of the month. You can sow early carrots, beetroot, broad beans, runner/stick beans, celery, leeks and turnips. These will germinate even in an unheated greenhouse.

Put seed potatoes in a tray (or better still, an egg tray or box) in a cool, light place to "chit" (see chapter 3).

On your window ledge (which is quite a bit warmer), you can sow herb seeds – parsley, sage, thyme, mint. If you are planning to grow them in a greenhouse or minigreenhouse, you can also plant tomato seeds. But if they are to go outdoors eventually, leave this till next month, as the plants will get too big too soon.

Outdoors

You can plant out early potatoes, but they will still have to be covered with cloches or fleece for about a month.

If you didn't do it in January, cover the ground with polythene or tunnel cloches to warm the soil up for early crops. If the weather is harsh, it might be useful to cover any outdoor strawberries with cloches or fleece for protection against frosts.

To help any fruit trees or vegetables which are overwintering, you can give them a good top-dressing of home-made compost or farmyard manure. Around winter crops, it is best if the manure is not too fresh. If it is fresh, leave it in a heap for a couple of weeks in the cold and then apply it.

March

This is where the work really starts! The ground should begin to warm up, even in the coolest areas. Apply the hedgerow test (chapter 5) before planting young vegetables out into the garden or their outdoor containers. (Actually container growing can get a real boost here, as you can plant up the container and keep it under cover until you are ready, then move the whole thing out into its growing place.)

Indoors

Sow tomatoes, peppers, cucumbers, courgettes, marrows and squash. Also, make second sowings of peas and beans if you want a succession and have the space outside.

Previously sown seeds (e.g. tomato, pepper, cucumber) will probably need potting on into small, and then slightly larger, pots or containers.

In milder areas, you may be able to start hardening off (chapter 3) the young plants, and in very mild areas, you could be planting out the first vegetables by the end of the month. BUT – and it is a big but – do watch out for late frosts. March can be a treacherous month, and a sudden late frost can kill young plants and waste all your work to date. If frost is forecast, bring the plants indoors for the odd night, or cover them with plastic or fleece, just until the risk has passed.

Continue to transplant the squash, cucumbers, tomatoes and peppers, and possibly start hardening off the outdoor varieties towards the end of the month.

Start off the seeds of cauliflower, brussels sprouts and cabbage.

Outdoors

Plant onion sets, shallots and early potatoes.

In milder areas you may be able to plant peas and beans directly outside for successional growing. In cooler areas you may have to wait to do this till towards the end of the month. Broad beans and hardened off runner/stick beans should be reasonably safe.

You may be able to try early sowings of salad – lettuce, radish, spring onions – and, certainly, all areas should be warm enough by the end of the month.

Plant new strawberry plants. Protect with fleece if there is a danger of frost. If growing in hanging baskets, it is probably easier to plant up the basket now, but leave it under cover and hang out next month.

April

The only real problem you may encounter now is rain. If the "April showers" turn out to be continuous downpours, the ground will be kept very cool, as well as wet. If you have drainage problems and the ground gets waterlogged, gently fork it over and add more drainage material (grit, compost, sharp sand or similar) before planting. But, if you do get genuine showers, then the growing conditions will be just right.

Indoors

Plant a second or third sowing of peas and beans. Begin purple sprouting broccoli, celery, leeks, cabbage and cauliflower. (These can be slow to germinate, so do not panic if they don't show very quickly.)

Pot up tomatoes, peppers and cucumbers.

On your window ledge or in the greenhouse if it is warm, sow parsley, dill, marjoram, chives and other slightly exotic herbs. They, too, are slow germinators, so patience is the order of the day.

Outdoors

If you haven't started them off indoors, sow seeds of pea, beans, carrot, beetroot, main crop potatoes and salad. Provide peas and runner and French beans with support.

Earth up the early potatoes, whether in containers or open soil.

Begin the watch for pests, as this is when the slugs and snails start to be a nuisance. You have to decide whether to kill them or simply remove them. If you choose the latter, they must be taken a least a mile away from your garden to be effective (they are great travellers). Remember, you will also attract pests from other gardens, with your promise of lovely, young food, so control is a non-stop job! If you choose to dispose permanently, see appendix 2.

May

By now your crops should be well under way. Pests are going to become more abundant with the warmer weather, so be vigilant for slugs and snails, cabbage white butterfly eggs (on undersides of leaves), carrot root fly and aphids.

If you have not used the whole of a packet of seed, you can probably keep the rest till next year (except for parsnip, which does not keep). Seal the packet carefully; put it in a glass jar, metal box or similar container (preferably not plastic, as it sweats and mice can chew through it); and store in a cool, dark place.

Indoors

The greenhouse will be coming into its own as a growing area, as well as an early plant nursery. Tomatoes, peppers and cucumbers which you are planning to grow indoors should need potting up again, as they grow until they are about 6–8"/15–20 cm tall and the roots fill the pot.

Prepare the final growing area – either a patch of soil, pots, bags or containers of your choice. Add compost or additional non-peat soil if needed, and put the supports in place. (Remember: tomato plants can grow to 6'/2 m and will require sturdy supports which are tall enough to take the whole adult plant.)

Towards the end of the month, you can begin planting tomatoes into their final growing space.

If planning to grow them outdoors, harden off tomatoes, cucumbers and herbs gently throughout the month, with a view to planting outdoors in ***June.***

Outdoors

Water may be an issue this month. May can be quite dry as well as warm. If there is no rain for three days, water all young vegetables each day until it next rains.

Further vegetables can be sown directly into the ground, if you wish. Also sow more delicate types (e.g. pumpkins, squash and summer salads).
Earth up potatoes again. If they are in open ground, make sure none are poking out at the side of the mound.

Parsley, fennel, coriander and dill can also be sown outside now.

Keep all crops free of weeds.

June

Now your work should be beginning to pay off, by providing food. Early salad, peas and broad beans will be harvestable. Early potatoes may be ready, though this is more likely in warmer parts only. Strawberries should be doing well, though.

Indoors

Monitor the tomatoes, peppers and cucumbers in the greenhouse. Tie them to the supports as they grow, and pinch out side shoots on tomatoes and feed them (see appendix 1) every two weeks.

If the greenhouse gets too hot, damp down the floor to raise the humidity and reduce the temperature a little. If it's not hot enough (the summer of 2007 in UK), be sure the door stays closed or your plants will stop growing temporarily and be slow to produce flowers (it's not fatal but does make it longer till you get fruits).

Outdoors

Continue transplanting young broccoli (and replacing any plants decimated by the slugs) and outdoor tomatoes and cucumbers. Also, any winter vegetables started in the greenhouse should be hardened off and planted into their growing spaces at the end of the month (cauliflower, cabbage, leeks, brussels sprouts).

Continue successional sowings of salad and herbs. If the earlier sown herbs are growing well, trim them gently and store either dried or frozen for later (see chapter 6).

Sow maincrop carrots and potatoes, if the weather is reasonably warm. Harvest peas, beans, carrots, salad and potatoes – and enjoy!

July

A relatively easy month, as most of the gardening work is maintenance – weeding, pest control, watering as necessary and harvesting.

Indoors

The greenhouse crops will only need more of the same maintenance as last month – pinching out side shoots, watering and feeding.

Outdoors

Sow maincrop carrots and potatoes if you didn't do it last month.
Top dress vegetables, particularly the younger winter ones, with well-rotted manure, compost or even grass clippings to preserve the moisture and give them a slow boost.

Tidy the strawberry plants and remove all dead foliage. If there are runners being produced, propagate new plants from these by pegging them into a separate small pot of compost until roots form; then cut the runner and allow the new plant to grow independently.

Do not let the vegetables dry out. Water regularly and thoroughly in dry weather. Runner beans in particular are at risk, as they are now large plants supporting a weight of fruits. If they dry out, they will stop producing flowers, and so, no further beans.

Some herbs may be producing flowers and seeds. Collect the seeds for next year. Pick the stems when the seed heads are turning brown and place in a paper bag somewhere cool. After a few weeks, check out the contents – the seeds will probably be separated from the pod (if not, shake very gently). Remove the pod husks and store the seeds in an envelope in your seed store.

Watch out for potato blight on maincrop potatoes (see chapter 7). Continue the fight against pests.

August

Another largely maintenance month. Harvesting the crops should be well under way now – a great job for the children.

Remember to harvest when the vegetables are at their best, rather than when you can use them. Crops left on the plant for later will get tougher or drier (or both), so it is better to pick all that are ready and store the excess until later (see individual chapter for methods).

Indoors

Tomatoes and peppers should be cropping now and the plants will be carrying a weight of fruits. Make sure the supports are sound and keep feeding every two weeks at least. Keep watering steadily (see chapter 5).
It is not too late to start off winter crops, if your schedule has got a bit behindhand. Sow spring cabbage, cauliflower and leeks.

Outdoors

More of the same – weeding, watering when needed, removing pests and monitoring plants for problems. General maintenance, in fact.
If you have the space, you can start off the winter crops outside instead of in the greenhouse. They will take slightly longer to germinate, and it is advisable to give them some protection against birds (cloches or fleece).

Plant on any strawberry runners which have made roots, and carry on potting out more if you want them. Otherwise, cut off the excess runners as you tidy the plants.

If you haven't done so already, provide a space or container for the compost heap. You will need it next month.

September

Now we begin planning for winter and next spring. If you are starting from scratch, begin to dig or prepare your ground for planting. Add manure or compost as necessary.

There will be quite a lot of waste now from the plants, so have the compost heap prepared to receive it. You will probably be cutting down peas and beans (remember to leave the roots in the ground and simply dig them in or let them rot into the soil). There may be early leaf drop if the weather has been dry. Collect them up for the compost rather than leave them amongst the vegetables, as they will provide a superb hiding place for slugs and other nuisances.

Indoors

Stop feeding tomatoes and peppers, but continue watering. Harvest whilst ever the weather is mild. Once is it obvious that the crops are not ripening, collect everything and ripen elsewhere (see chapter 5).

Once the growing crops are removed, the greenhouse can be cleaned ready for the next sowings.

Outdoors

Mainly harvesting and clearing.

Leave outdoor tomatoes on the plant for as long as possible, then bring indoors, like the greenhouse varieties.

Plant out spring cabbage, overwintering onions, broad bean and leek plants (as well, celery and cauliflower, if not done previously).

If you have raspberries and currants which have finished fruiting, they can be pruned and tidied towards the end of the month. Raspberries will need re-tying, as you will be cutting off the parts which were supported. Check the supports, and mend or replace as necessary. If you are just starting, buy and plant new canes and bushes now for next year.

Fruit trees – apples, pears and plums – can be planted now, either in open ground or containers. If in containers, do water regularly – every day if it doesn't rain – until the trees are established.

New rhubarb crowns can be planted. Give them plenty of manure or compost to grow into. Established crowns need to be tidied of any last leaves and then covered with a bucketful of compost or farm manure. Leave till the spring – the plant will do the rest.

If you have been leaving some crops to produce seeds, now is probably the last chance to collect them, before the autumn winds claim them.

October

You are now preparing for winter. Harvest the last of the crops and store or preserve them. Clear rubbish to the compost heap. Dig over any areas which need attention, and add compost as necessary.

Indoors

Bring tender herbs (e.g. dill, parsley) in to the window ledge to prolong their growing season. The greenhouse might be adequate at the beginning of the month but will be too cold for them by the end (unless you are heating it).

Begin sowing seeds of winter lettuce, baby spinach and possibly early carrots to have early crops from the greenhouse. Mange-Tout peas may also do well and are worth a try.

Outdoors

Watch out for frosts. The existing fruit trees and vegetable plants which have been in the open for a while should be safe, but newly planted vegetables may be at risk. If in doubt, give them a bit of protection.

Outdoor strawberries can be put in their growing area. If you planning to grow them in hanging baskets, it is better to put them into individual pots and store them in a sheltered spot. This is also better for the strawberries you grew this summer. Hanging baskets are a bit too shallow for long-term growing, so better practice is to remove the plants, pot them up and return to the basket next spring. If you are storing in the greenhouse, don't forget to water them occasionally through the winter.

You can still plant spring cabbage and onions. Garlic can be planted now, too.

The brussels sprouts plants should be quite big now, so make sure they have sufficient support and are firmly in the ground. If necessary, press round them with your heel to firm them up (loose soil will definitely reduce the crop).

If it's not too cold, you can still plant fruit trees.

November

You are really beginning to wind down, now. Most crops should be gently doing their own thing – you job is to ensure they are not damaged by the weather.

Indoors

You may be able to continue growing winter salad and herbs in an unheated greenhouse in milder areas. Otherwise, either heat the greenhouse or bring the crops indoors to a window ledge. Most herbs will continue growing through most of the winter, indoors with modern central heating, provided they have enough light.

Outdoors

Monitor the *Brassica*s, celery, broad beans, garlic and other overwintering crops for weather damage. Give support where necessary.
If you haven't already done so, you can plant fruit trees and raspberry canes, whilst the soil remains fairly loose and unfrozen.

If you still have carrots and parsnips in the ground or containers, dig them up now and store them (they are not going to get any better).

You may find small colonies of snails or slugs collecting in covered areas, cracks in walls or under heaps, to hibernate for the winter. This is good chance to dispose of them in numbers and make next spring easier.

If you have plenty of compost or manure, you can top dress the established fruit trees and bushes. Just give them a good, thick layer around the stem, and leave nature to do the rest.

New beds or areas can be dug over roughly, ready for planting next spring. You can leave the soil in quite big lumps, as the frosts will beak it down in time and the cold can get at pests more easily than if the soil is level.

December

Another relatively easy month.

You will be harvesting sprouts, cabbage, cauliflower and leeks as you need them. There may well be some winter salad left in the greenhouse or on your window ledge.

If the weather is pleasant and the soil isn't frozen, you can continue winter digging as necessary. You can also still plant fruit trees, though this is about the limit for doing this.

On the whole, you can enjoy reading all the new season's catalogues and planning for spring, and curl up with all those great gardening books everyone bought you for Christmas and dream of crops to come.

Enjoy!

DOWN TO EARTH

Appendix 1

Beneficial additions to help growth

1. Garden compost

Home-made compost produced from all organic waste is the very best food for your crops. Apply as a mulch during the winter – a good thick layer, say 2–4"/5–10 cm – or dig into newly turned soil when preparing a bed or area for planting.

2. Farmyard manure

The best manure of all is from horses, but cattle- and pig-produced products are quite acceptable. Do not apply directly round existing plants, trees or shrubs, as it will be too strong and could produce enough heat to actually damage the plants. Add to compost heap or pile up separately for a few weeks to let it rot down before putting it on the ground. You can buy commercial, ready-composted farmyard manures, if you are in a hurry, but straight from the farm is best (and often free).

Chicken manure is more expensive, but very effective. Fresh droppings from the chicken (if you can get them) are extremely strong and MUST be composted for some time before using. Commercial variations, usually ready-composted, are easier and cleaner to use and provide a good boost.

Intensive (battery) reared chicken droppings are not suitable.

If the source of any of these products is not organic, compost the droppings for about six months before use.

3. Mushroom compost

This is the waste from commercial mushroom cultivation, and is usually based on farmyard manure, soil and composted additives known to the mushroom grower. It is ready-composted, having been used once for the mushrooms, and usually fine and easy to mix with your soil or home-made compost. Although used once, it usually retains a high degree of fertility as well as acting as a soil improver.

If the source is not organic, compost, as above.

4. Blood, fish and bone

This is a long-established fertiliser, made from the waste from meat processing. It comes in powder form, is easy to apply and is a good slow-release general fertiliser.

This can be added directly to the soil, even round existing crops. But take care not to let it cling to the plants themselves – it is a little powerful for direct use.

The downside is that it smells and tastes of meat, so your dogs and cats will love it! It is probably best to gently fork it into the top of the soil to avoid the temptation to your animals.

If you are vegetarian or vegan, this product is not for you.

5. Hoof and horn

A similar product to the previous, but made from different parts of the animals. Use in the same way.

6. Fish meal

As above, but from the fish industry, rather than animals. It is preferable that the products are not from fish reared intensively – check the source.

7. Seaweed

Seaweed extract is produced commercially in a powder or liquid form. Both types are a very good growth-boost. They can be put in the soil when you plant out, or scattered as a top-dressing for growing crops. They are a really good aid to growing.

If you live near the sea, seaweed from the shore is just as effective. Add to the compost heap or collect separately – leave for a number of weeks before use to lose the salt which may be on it. (On some beaches, you must get permission to collect, and, in any case, you can only take dead seaweed brought up by the tide.)

8. Sewage sludge

Yes, you can! It will be available already treated, de-odourised and packaged. Check out your local treatment works or water provider for details.

9. Wood ash

The ashes from a bonfire or barbecue will provide a general soil improver. Although not high in fertiliser, they provide trace elements, such as potassium, which are beneficial.

10. Home-made liquid feeds

Generally, liquid feeds are used on plants grown in containers or a similarly restricted environment. They can be used on general, open-ground planting, but are usually unnecessary if the soil is being fed with other products.

You can make your own feeds for your plants from a variety of products. The basic method is to soak the product in a bucket or tub of water for about four weeks. The resultant liquid is drained off, diluted further (50–50) and then applied to the crops.

It is probably easier to handle if the products are in a hessian sack or similar, but not essential for the result.

You can use farmyard manure (about two spades full to a bag), rhubarb leaves, nettles, camomile or alfalfa.

NB. All the resultant liquids are very smelly. Don't be put off – they are very beneficial.

If you don't already use the water from boiled vegetables for gravy or sauces, why not give it to your plants? Allow to cool, then either water plants directly or pour on to the compost.

11. Green manures

If you have a large patch of land and/or time, you can use green manures in advance of planting. These are crops which are planted, then dug into the soil, to provide trace elements, particularly nitrogen.

You can plant alfalfa, clover, mustard, tares, field beans or fenugreek. All are sown directly into the ground, grown until just before the flowers appear and then dug into the soil to rot down in situ. They must be dug in at least one month before you wish to sow your crops, and a bit longer if possible.

12. Commercial manures and fertilisers

Provided these products are made from organic sources (check for RHS, HDRA or similar organic symbols), they are quite acceptable. The only downside is the cost.

DOWN TO EARTH

Appendix 2

Coping organically with pests and diseases

Once your growing area is established, the balance of predators and prey will keep most of your produce relatively safe. This will take anything up to six years. In the meantime, and particularly with a new growing area, you will have various "nasties" to ward off to protect your crops. Here some acceptable, organic solutions to common problems.

1. Slugs and snails

a) *Removal* is the only way to protect your crops without killing the animal. Simply collect the slugs or snails, place in a suitably deep container, such as a bucket (any shallower and you will spend a lot of time pushing them back in), carry at least one mile away and release. Yes, they can travel a mile and will head back to your lovely fresh crops, so the further the better.

b) *Squashing* is a simple though slightly messy system. Simply squash the creature underfoot or with the back of a spade or trowel. Bury the resultant mess in the garden or add to the compost heap. It is easier to squash on a hard surface, such as a path, but the mess will make it slippery, so do clear up afterwards.

c) *Very salty water.* See chapter 2 – remember the water must be very salty to be effective.

d) *Nematodes* are tiny, wormlike, parasitic creatures which are natural predators to slugs and snails. They can be bought from various suppliers on the Internet, and are applied by watering onto the growing area. They only attack slugs so are harmless to other creatures and the crops. They are affected by temperature, so use as the instructions in warmer (preferably damp) weather.

e) *Natural predators* can be encouraged into the garden to help in the fight. Chief eaters of snails are thrushes and blackbirds. They will remove a good number in the course of a season, so should be encouraged into the area with water, perching places (a high wall or fence is ideal) and possibly winter feeding.

Frogs and toads will also take slugs, particularly young ones. You will need a pond to encourage them to come into your area.

Slow worms and other small lizards are excellent predators. They will need somewhere to hide in between foraging in your growing spaces. You may well find them in the compost heap (a favourite of the slow worms in my garden), under stones, under dense clumps of plants (e.g. geranium or aubrietia). They are quite harmless to anything other than slugs.

Smaller predators, such as centipedes and ground beetles, will eat the eggs and young of slugs.

f) *Beer traps* are effective if slightly expensive. Basically, they are containers three-quarters full of beer (or similar) or water. The slugs and snails are attracted by the liquid, but drown because it is too deep to cope with. A container such as a 599g margarine or yoghurt tub is ideal for

for this purpose – simply bury it till the rim is level with the soil, and empty out the bodies and refill as necessary (possibly daily if the problem is a big one). The bodies and liquid can go onto the compost heap.

A variation on the trap is the "slug moat". Use lengths of guttering, sunk into the soil as previously, to completely surround the growing area (mitre the end and join together with some silicon sealant or similar). Fill with water (beer really would be too expensive!) and dispose of the bodies as before.

g) *Barriers*, in the form of cloches or fleece, can be put round young plants till they are string enough to resist.

h) *Slug pellets* are not encouraged, as they get into the food chain and affect the natural predators in turn. There are some organic forms of pellet on the market, but you are advised to check these out thoroughly and look for any approved symbols (HDRA or Soil Association) on the packaging.

2. Aphids

a) *Squashing* is the simplest and most effective way of removing aphids from your plants, especially if you catch them early before the infestation is too big. Simply run your thumb and index finger upwards along the stem or bud, gently squeezing as you go. Repeat till all are squashed. Wear rubber gloves if you don't fancy the feel of the activity.

b) *Natural predators* are legion. All the following should be encouraged into your area, as they will be real allies – ladybirds (ladybugs/pasca bugs), lacewings, hoverflies, spiders, and capsid bugs.

c) *Sprays* are to be used only where necessary, not as a regular items – most will affect beneficial insects as well as the aphids. The following are acceptable for occasional use: pyrethrum (made from marigold flowers); insecticidal soap; derris. All should be sprayed directly on to the aphids on the plant. They will not act as a deterrent by being sprayed prior to the aphids arriving.

On crops such as broad beans, aphids (usually blackfly) are unsightly, but do little damage unless they totally coat the plant. Nipping off the tip of the plant, where the infestation usually starts, is often enough to stop it.

3. Fungal diseases

a) *Bordeaux mixture* can be used to alleviate peach leaf curl, apple scab and potato blight. This is a compound of copper and sulphur, which can be applied to crops to prevent or contain the infection. If the infection is very localised, simply remove the infected parts and burn them (do not add to the compost heap); in any case, spray whilst the infection is showing the early blotches (once the leaves have curled, the spray cannot reach the spores, so is useless). Always spray carefully, in still weather. Evening is best, as the bees will have stopped working.

b) *Good garden ventilation* is probably the best way to avoid fungal diseases. Warm, damp conditions encourage the fungal spores to form, so ensure the air can circulate round the plants, and avoid overwatering (particularly with potatoes – see chapter 7).

❦ Find out more: ❦

www.downtoearthinternational.co.uk

pcparr@btinmternet.com

Sources of organic seeds:

      UK: Living foods of St Ives;

            www.sprouting seeds.co,uk;

      US: Caudill seeds inc.;

            www.caudilseed.com

Sprout people L.A.

            www.sproutpeople.com

Johnny's Selected Seeds

            www.johnnyseeds.com

Tamar organics

            www.tamarorganics.co.uk

Seeds of Italy

            www.seedsofitaly.com

Useful websites:

The Soil Association: www.soilassociation.org

Royal Horticultural Society: www.rhs.org.uk

Henry Doubleday Research Association: www.gardenorganic.org.uk

Kitchen Gardeners International: www.kitchengardeners.org

Further reading:

Not on the Label
Felicity Lawrence

It isn't Easy Being Green
Dick Strawbridge

The Big Earth Book
James Bruges

The Little Food Book
Craig Sams

One Planet Living

Pooran Desai and Paul King

Encyclopaedia of Organic Gardening
Henry Doubleday Research Association

Bob Flowerdew's Organic Bible
Bob Flowerdew

Bring Me My Bow
John Seymour